CHILD OF THE REVOLUTION

MECHANICS-
MERCANTILE
LIBRARY.

Arthur F Mathews '06

CHILD OF THE REVOLUTION

GROWING UP IN CASTRO'S CUBA

LUIS M. GARCIA

ALLEN&UNWIN

First published in 2006

Copyright © Luis M. Garcia 2006

Map by Ian Faulkner

Allen & Unwin
83 Alexander Street
Crows Nest NSW 2065
Australia
Phone: (61 2) 8425 0100
Fax: (61 2) 9906 2218
Email: info@allenandunwin.com
Web: www.allenandunwin.com

National Library of Australia
Cataloguing-in-Publication entry:

Garcia, Luis M., 1959– .
  Child of the revolution : growing up in Castro's Cuba.

  ISBN 1 74114 852 9.

  1. Garcia, Luis M., 1959– . 2. Children – Cuba – Social conditions. 3. Cubans – Australia – Biography. 4. Cuba – Politics and government – 1959–1990. I. Title.

972.91064092

Set in 12/16 pt Bembo by Midland Typesetters, Australia
Printed by Griffin Press, Adelaide

10 9 8 7 6 5 4 3 2 1

To Isabel, Carmen and Javier
And to my parents

And to every parent who has had to choose exile

CONTENTS

To be Cuban is to go with Cuba everywhere.
Cuba is a paradise from which we flee by trying to return.

GUILLERMO CABRERA INFANTE

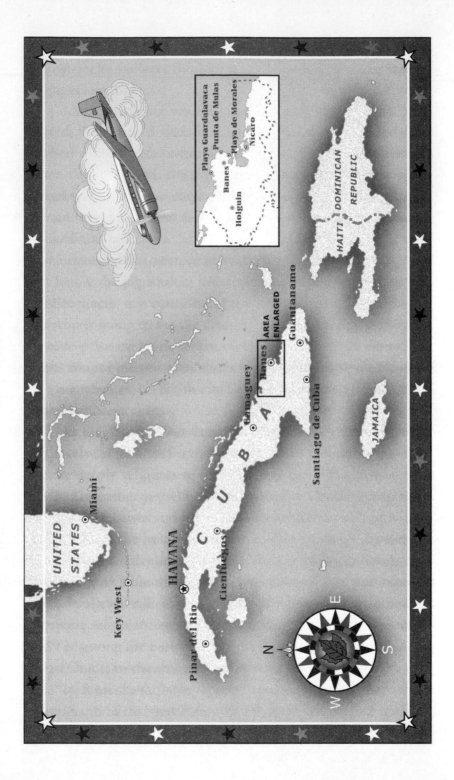

1 · DON'T LOOK BACK...

Don't look back. Whatever you do, don't look back. Because even at the last minute, even as you walk up the stairs into the plane, if you look back just once—just once!—and they see you looking back, they will *know* you don't want to leave Cuba and then they will bring you down those steps, *chico*, and they will keep you in Cuba. Your parents will go, but you will stay. You will *never* see them again. So, pay attention: whatever you do, *no mires para atrás!* Don't look back!

I am sitting on one of the hard stone benches that ring the promenade around the Parque Cárdenas, which used to be the municipal pride of Banes *antes del Triunfo* but now looks a little unloved. I am listening to one of my best friends, Pepito. He is older than I am, not by much, true, but somehow he seems to know so much more than I do. And he is the one who is explaining to me why, now that my family is finally being allowed to leave Cuba—nearly three years after we applied, Pepito, nearly three years!—why I cannot, under any circumstances, even hint that I may not want to leave with them. Look back, he repeats, and they will keep you here. These are words that instil absolute fear in my twelve year old heart.

Pepito and I are talking just hours after the news arrived at home. I don't know who brought it, but I heard my mother say something about the police. Whoever it was, they came knocking on our door with *el telegrama* while my brother and I were at school. This telegram, this magical, mythical telegram, contains the news we have been desperately waiting for since mid 1968— permission from Fidel Castro to leave Cuba. At least I think it's from Fidel. Everything in Cuba is decided by Fidel, according to my father, so I can just imagine *El Máximo Líder*, as he is always called in the newspaper and on radio, sitting there in his palace in Havana, going through piles of applications from people begging for permission to leave his workers' paradise. Fidel sits there and with a deep sigh signs our permission slip. Let them pack their meagre belongings and leave. Good riddance, I can hear him say, chewing on those fat cigars he still smoked back then. Good riddance . . .

Everyone who applies to leave Cuba waits, sometimes for three years, sometimes for five, sometimes forever, for Fidel to finally agree to let you leave. And during that time, from the moment you apply to leave to the moment when *el telegrama* arrives, you become a *gusano*. A counter-revolutionary who is made to pay in all sorts of subtle and not so subtle ways for the audacity of asking permission to leave. Of course, I know that once you are given permission to leave, you are not coming back. Fidel said so himself: if you leave Cuba, you are a traitor and you are never coming back. Never.

As soon as we applied for permission, my father was sent to the labour camps where all *gusanos* get sent, to cut sugarcane for the Revolution, and for a long time we only got to see him once every forty-five days when he was given a five-day pass. But

2

I am sure someone there, the camp commander or someone in authority, has broken the news to him that *el telegrama* has arrived. I picture my father acting normally, as if nothing has happened, just in case the guards think he is too happy about leaving Cuba and decide to keep him back for another few months. But inside, I know he is jumping for joy.

My mother is jumping for joy inside, too, I figure, although you can't tell for sure. Her eyes are red from crying and I know there will be more tears, many more to come over the next two or three days before we finally leave Banes. Who wants to leave their family behind? She worries about her sisters and her brothers who are staying in Cuba. They are in enough trouble as it is for being related to *gusanos* . . .

Everyone in our street seems to know about the telegram. Our neighbours next door. The Tavera sisters across the road, who are really like family. Everyone has heard about *el telegrama de los García*. I know that some of the neighbours will pop by later in the day, when it gets dark, to say congratulations in hushed, counter-revolutionary tones and wish us luck, but others, like the woman who is the boss of the neighbourhood Committee for the Defence of the Revolution—the one we call *La Compañera*—will be watching, and muttering under her breath. *Hijos de puta*, she probably says. Good riddance.

As I sit talking to Pepito, it hits me that this may be one of the last times I will see my friends, the park at the end of the street where we live, the neighbours, the basketball courts across the park . . . So much for celebrating. But I can't look back. I know that much. Besides, there is so much to do. Now the telegram has arrived, we have just three days to finalise the documents we need to fly out, pack our stuff, and leave Banes for Havana where, God and Fidel willing, we will board the plane for Madrid. Not that there is much to pack. My mother told my eleven year old brother and me that the instructions from the police were clear: we are allowed to take just the one suitcase per person. No more. That's the rule. It's the paperwork that will take all that time. And saying goodbye, of course.

The first to arrive the very next day are the police—the *milicianos*. Again. Except this time we are expecting them. When you apply for permission to leave Cuba—when you fill in the application form that will change your life forever—you get a visit from the police. Sometimes accompanied by someone from the Committee for the Defence of the Revolution, they set about taking written stock of everything in the house. It's called *pasar balance*. A stocktake for *gusanos*. They note down every single thing in your house—the number and style of plates, the number of cups and saucers in the pantry, the television set in the lounge room (we should be so lucky!), the ironing board, your jewellery, if you have any. Everything, regardless of monetary or sentimental value. It's all noted down in great detail because these goods no longer belong to you. They are the property of the People. They belong to the Revolution. You can use them between now and the day you get the telegram saying you can leave Cuba, but you cannot sell them or barter them or do anything with them. Because when the telegram arrives, the police will come again with their clipboards and pencils and make sure every single item listed on their forms remains behind in Cuba. It's the property of the People. If anything is missing, who knows what will happen?

So, the *milicianos* have come to complete their task. There are two of them—the more senior one, whose name is Morgado, is known to my parents. This is Banes, after all, a small, unpretentious town where everyone knows everyone else. The *milicianos* are polite and, I sense, a little confused, but painfully efficient when it comes to the paperwork. I am sure their instructions are clear—

4

make life hell for these ungrateful *gusanos*. Make them pay. But this is Banes, so instead they don't say much, politely ticking away at their list of possessions, plate by plate, while my mother watches anxiously.

Since applying to leave Cuba, we have been extra careful with the plates and the glasses and the big American-made radio in the dining room. When a plate smashed in the kitchen many months ago, my mother picked up the pieces, carefully wrapped them up in newspaper and put the package at the back of the cupboard for safekeeping. Same with the glasses. Same with everything. Now, I see her unwrap the yellowing pages of the papers, one by one, showing the broken china to these two policemen, making sure they know it's all there. I think she cries as she does this. I am not sure. I know she is dead scared that one of the *milicianos* will pause and then place a cross instead of a tick on his list. Just like that. A cross instead of a tick, and then we will have to stay in Cuba.

2 · IN A TIME OF REVOLUTION

Leaving Cuba seems like a totally crazy, totally foreign idea to my parents on this warm Friday, 10 July 1959, as my mother, lying back on an operating bed at the Hospital Civil de Banes, legs up in stirrups, face contorted by pain, pushes and yells and pushes some more to get me out of her womb and into the world. It's been a long labour—nearly twenty-four hours—and she is exhausted, but she knows it's not over yet, so she keeps pushing, holding on to the midwife, imploring her doctor, Edmundo Prieto, to put an end to the pain, *¡por favor!* Instead, he whispers soothing words of encouragement: One more push, the doctor says. Almost there, *señora* . . .

My father is not in the delivery room. He is Cuban and Cuban men don't attend the birth of a child because, well—do I need to tell you that this is women's work? No, no, like most men of his generation, he has been waiting outside, smoking cigarette after cigarette, not knowing what is going on inside but silently praying to the patron saint of Cuba, the Virgen de la Caridad del Cobre, that everything works out all right, because when you are in trouble in Cuba, or even when you are just worried about something, you always pray to the Virgen de la Caridad del Cobre.

Eventually, the nurses will come out into the corridor and tell my father that everything is fine and then they will let him come into the room to have a look at his tired but beaming wife and his newborn son, and he will shake hands with Dr Prieto and, as is customary, invite the doctor to join him and his friends for a few celebratory drinks. In fact, my father's friends have started celebrating already, down at Bar Feria, a small bar in Bayamo Street that is just a few minutes' walk from the modest but promising haberdashery shop my parents own in the main street of Banes. They will celebrate until the late, late hours, drinking dark rum, top shelf, of course, for this is a special occasion. Later on, as the huge American jukebox in the corner keeps being fed coins so it can keep playing those syrupy Vicentico Valdez *boleros* that are all the rage in Cuba, there will be plenty of Cristal and Hatuey beers and everyone will be smoking big, fat Partagas cigars that have been purchased by my proud father to mark the birth of his first boy. After all, there is much to celebrate in Banes, and not just the arrival of a son.

It has been six months since President Fulgencio Batista fled Havana, unceremoniously chased out by a few hundred bearded guerrillas who had spent the previous three years fighting high up in the Sierra Maestra mountains, in the far eastern region of the country. Around midnight on New Year's Eve 1958, Batista packed up his family, his closest friends and suitcases said to be bulging with cash, and went into exile, to the delight of most Cubans. Within hours the *barbudos*, as the rebels are known, take over the island, captivating an entire nation—and quite a few on the outside—with their unkempt beards, olive green fatigues and prominent crucifixes hanging around their necks.

This revolution, the latest in a long list of often futile rebellions and uprisings going back over a century, is led by a young lawyer called Fidel Castro, the son of a Spanish-born landowner in Oriente province. He is known by everyone as Fidel because when you know someone well in Cuba, you always use their first name, and he is now running things in Havana, not from the Presidential Palace where all previous presidents and dictators have settled, but from his new headquarters in, of all places, the American-owned Havana Hilton Hotel, which has been renamed, with much fanfare, the *Habana Libre*—the Free Havana. Like the names of hotels and streets and parks, Cuba is about to change forever, in ways that neither my father nor his happily intoxicated friends at Bar Feria can even begin to realise.

The winds of change are certainly picking up strength by July: over the past six months, the casinos in Havana have been taken over by the new revolutionary government and their American owners of dubious reputation have fled back to Miami or Las Vegas. Rents have been cut in half and electricity and telephone charges will also be reduced significantly. What's more, it seems the big, foreign-owned utilities are happy to go along with the *barbudos*, at least for now. In a show of goodwill to the new governing class, they have offered to pay their taxes in full—and in advance. Meanwhile, former Batista supporters, now stripped of their uniforms and their power, are being tried by military tribunals in spectacles that are televised live every night from the largest sports stadium in Havana, where thousands of audience members stamp their feet and yell out, *Paredón, paredón*—To the firing squad—even before the military judges have decided whether the accused is guilty or not, which doesn't matter much because everyone in Cuba knows they are guilty.

Fidel himself, always wearing green fatigues, appears at the televised trials every now and then, sometimes even questioning the accused. As the crowds chant, Fidel! Fidel! Fidel!, he promises that the trials will continue until all the criminals of the Batista regime are brought to justice, regardless of criticism from lawyers and human rights activists in the United States and Europe. Fidel has kept his promise made in the Sierra Maestra and seized large land-holdings, including those owned by American companies, divided them up and is handing over small parcels of land— precious, fertile Cuban land—to *campesinos* who appear on television wearing big hats, missing teeth and crying in gratitude. Everyone expects Fidel to keep another of his key promises: to hold free and fair elections within eighteen months.

And here in Banes, a small sugar town some fifteen hours by road from Havana, there is plenty of support for the *barbudos*. Not from everyone, though: the town is home to dozens of American families, who are getting nervous about some of the anti-American pronouncements coming from the new leadership. There are some Cuban families, too, rich and well-known families like the Diaz Balarts and the Cárdenas, who are quietly packing up their bags for the short plane flight across to Miami. But most people think Fidel is on the right track, including my normally apolitical parents, who think politics is a dirty game best left to the professionals. They are pretty hopeful, like most other Cubans, that things are about to get better.

One way or another, every family in Cuba has been touched by the fighting of the past few years. My father's brother-in-law, my uncle Luis Felipe, had been working with the underground trade unions in the area, distributing anti-Batista pamphlets. On my mother's side, the involvement is just as personal: her oldest brother, my uncle Victor, made the trek up to the Sierra Maestra to join the *barbudos* about two years ago. Neither my mother nor her sisters knew for sure whether he was dead or alive until he, too, came down from the mountains as a liberator six months ago. After so many sleepless nights, his return was greeted by the family with great joy and much relief.

My uncle Tony, who works for an American mining company in the nearby town of Nicaro, also distributed anti-Batista propaganda. But my mother worried most about her youngest brother, my uncle Papi, who is barely out of his teens. He became involved in local demonstrations against Batista and came close to being sent to jail, where he would have been tortured and almost certainly murdered, according to my mother. It was a period of such anguish that, even when she talks about it nearly fifty years later, she becomes visibly upset. Terrible, she says, it was a terrible time.

My parents have been married for just twelve months, after what my mother's sisters describe as a whirlwind romance. The wedding was large and generous, at least by Banes standards. Since neither of my parents is a regular church-goer, the ceremony took place not in the local Catholic church but in the big old house that belongs to my mother's family, in the grandly named Presidente Zayas Avenue, which in reality is not much of an avenue but a very ordinary, unpaved road that turns into a river of mud every time it rains heavily. It's a timber house with a corrugated iron roof, where my mother and her sisters and her brothers grew up, where her father died a slow, terrible death from cancer long before I was born, where her mother, whom I never met either, died in agony soon after being diagnosed with severe pancreas problems. It's the type of house where the walls are scarred by family history and the rooms inhabited by far, far too many family ghosts. But on the day my parents marry, it is a happy house.

More than sixty relatives, neighbours and friends turn up to the wedding celebrations, the women wearing their brightest and finest dresses and the men in immaculate white linen suits and those thin ties that are so fashionable at this time, to toast the wedding of Gisela and Luis. The wedding even makes it into the local paper, *El Pueblo*, a brief item in the social pages that describes my mother in characteristically parochial terms as radiant and my father as an upstanding young man with a bright future. The celebration must have cost a bit of money, but no one seems to mind. Everyone is having far too good a time. There is plenty of beer and rum and tables groan under the weight of roast pork and *congrí*, a dish made from rice and black beans, and *yuca* and *malanga* tubers and plantain, and a big wedding cake, and when you look at the large, black and white photographs that are taken, you can see all my uncles and my aunts, on both sides of the family, and some of my cousins and my mother's friends, and everyone is enjoying themselves.

Since they married, my parents have been renting a semi-detached house in Flor Crombet Street, just a block from the Parque Cárdenas, one of two main parks in the town. The building is one big long timber house owned by a woman called Celestina, a widow of independent financial means, according to the neighbourhood, who has wisely decided to divide the large property into three self-contained houses and rent two of them out. Celestina, who must be in her sixties, lives in the middle house, which is the largest and most comfortable, with her son Rodrigo. Of indeterminate age, Rodrigo is obviously mentally ill, although no one in the street will ever talk about it openly because it's not polite. Poor Celestina, is all they ever say, shaking their heads.

My mother says Rodrigo goes through stages—sometimes he is almost normal, she says, but most of the time we can tell that he is not. We don't see or hear him much because he is usually very quiet, but you can sense he is there, on the other side of the wall. Sometimes I am sure I can hear him breathe, and in years to come I will convince myself that if I try hard enough, I can even hear him think. Every now and then, when we least expect it, Rodrigo punches and kicks the walls separating our houses with such force and frustration that I jump up in the air, drop whatever I am doing and run to hide in the kitchen.

On the other side of Celestina, in a smaller house, live the Castros, who are described by everyone in the street as quiet, hardworking and polite, but with whom we don't socialise at all. It never occurs to me that it's because they are black. We just don't.

The house in Flor Crombet Street is not a place for a growing family by any means. There is a living area at the front, one bedroom, a dining area, a kitchen and then the bathroom, ending in a small yard devoid of any greenery except for the one lonesome coconut tree that will torment my mother for years to come, mischievously dropping its big, heavy coconuts seemingly at random but inevitably when she is outside. This is a temporary house for a young couple who dream of doing well in their small business. They are modest dreams. Already, my parents have started looking at empty blocks of land in town, including a block just next door to the family house on Presidente Zayas Avenue, but buying the land—it will be expensive—and then building a new house on the site will have to wait because now, in July 1959, my parents have other priorities, like a new son.

My father also has plans for the *Retacería García*, as their shop is called: he wants to expand the inventory and employ a couple of extra assistants. My mother is more cautious, thinking it best to consolidate first before expanding further. Like most girls of her generation, she never progressed past primary school—that was reserved for the boys—but when it comes to business, she is as sharp as a tack. Everyone in the family knows that. It's a trait most García women seem to have, and one their husbands tend to lack. Besides, she tells my father, there is just too much going on in Cuba at the moment. Let's wait. Let's not tempt fate.

She says she is not a superstitious woman, but even before she arrives home with her new son, five days after giving birth, she has pinned a small black amulet—an *azabache*—to my baby clothes because, like her mother before her, like her grandmother, like her sisters and like every other mother in Cuba, she knows full well that only a black *azabache* can protect your new baby from *mal de ojo*—the evil eye.

In July 1959 my parents' shop is modest but still manages to make enough money for my parents to have hired two employees. It's in the perfect spot, in the same block on General Marrero Street as other, larger department stores and next to a bank branch, so passing trade is not a problem. And like most other shopkeepers in town, my parents are happy to give credit, which means they have built up a loyal clientele, not just in town but in the surrounding sugarcane plantations and farmhouses, where there are lots of peasants—*guajiros*—with large families. It's good times in the *Retacería García* and good times in Banes.

But that is the type of town Banes has always been. Prosperous. At least that's one version of the history of Banes. It's the version I will hear some years later, when I am older. It will be told to me in hushed, conspiratorial tones by my mother's aunts, elderly women with white hair and wrinkled skin who smell of Spanish gardenia perfume. They are always talking about how things used to be before the Revolution—*antes del Triunfo*—much to the dismay of the rest of the family, who keep telling them to please, please, keep your voice down and stop all this crazy talk. *Dios santo*, do you want us all to end up in jail?

In the version told by my mother's aunts, Banes started as a small, poor fishing village known as La Ensanada, where a local family who were descendants of earlier French migrants, the Dumois, started growing big, sweet bananas for export to Europe. The banana plantations would be the start of modern Banes, attracting workers from the surrounding areas, small businesses and a modest amount of prosperity. It didn't last long. In the late 1890s, the town was razed to the ground by Cuban independence rebels fighting the Spaniards. Then, at the end of that century, the Spanish American War would see the once-great Spanish empire resoundingly defeated in Cuba by a newly emerging, powerful world player: the United States. Spain was forced to cede the ever-loyal Island of Cuba, as the colony was known, to the Americans. The Americans in turn stayed in Cuba as an occupying power until 1902, when the new Republic of Cuba was born, independent but closely watched from Washington.

It was at about that time that the United Fruit Company arrived in the Banes area, attracted by cheap land and easy access to the Bahia de Nipe, the largest bay in the country, and changed the place forever. Or at least until January 1959, when everything in Banes, and everything in Cuba, changed again. The United Fruit Company—which would become known to everyone in Banes simply as *La Compañía*—bought huge tracts of land in the district and started to grow sugarcane, lots of sugarcane, which was then cut by local Cubans during the harvesting months and sent for processing to two large sugar mills in the district, the Preston and the Boston. It was a hugely profitable enterprise for *La Compañía*. My mother's aunts tell me that this was the beginning of a golden age for Banes because *La Compañía* started building whole neighbourhoods for the American supervisors and their families, building new schools, new roads, new parks and public buildings. The Americans put Banes on the map, my mother's aunts say, their eyes lighting up with nostalgic excitement. It became the most American town in Cuba.

It meant that Banes was really divided in two: the American part of Banes, on one side of the River Banes, and on the other side the Cuban part of Banes, linked by a modest bridge. The American part of Banes was owned by *La Compañía*, and it had its own stores that were near-exact replicas of American shops, and its own schools and clubs, which were open only to those Cubans who were either well-off and could afford to buy their way in, or who worked for the United Fruit Company. The streets in the American part are wide and have large shady trees planted along the sidewalks, and the houses have lush tropical gardens at the front and big, leafy backyards. They have large, cool, enclosed verandas, timber floors and ceiling fans. Even mosquito nets. It's in the American part of Banes that one of my mother's aunts lives, her aunt Maria, whose husband Otto had a senior position at *La Compañía*.

Unlike the Americans, who left pretty soon after Fidel came to power, my mother's aunt and her husband stay put, at least until the mid 1960s, living in the same big, American style house that makes the house where we live look quite insignificant. I know about the American part of Banes because we visit my mother's aunt often and because, years later, when I am older, I will walk along the streets with the big shady trees on my way to my secondary school, which used to be known as *Los Amigos* because it was an American school run by the Quakers, but now has a different, revolutionary name, like everything else in Banes that was American *antes del Triunfo* but isn't any more.

Then there is the Cuban part of town, where we live, next to Celestina and her son who is mentally ill but, please, let's not talk about it. This part is older, the houses are smaller, very few have gardens at the front, and the streets don't have too many trees planted along the kerb. This part of Banes, the Cuban part, is where the main shops are and the church and the cinemas and

15

the town hall, a three-storey wedding cake of a building that is known to all in Banes by the much more fancy name of *El Palacio Municipal*. It's a different world, the Cuban side of Banes. Unlike the American side, which is quiet and green and tidy and odourless, on the Cuban side someone is always yelling at the top of their voice, calling their kids to dinner or gossiping with neighbours or at the corner store, and there are gangs of school children riding their bicycles along the footpaths or playing *pelota*—the Cuban version of baseball—right in the middle of the street. And there is the smell of food, Cuban food, with plenty of garlic and onions and a tomato *sofrito* which you make with fresh tomatoes and a little lemon or lime juice, and there is always music blaring from a radio somewhere, a sweet *mambo* that makes you feel happy and makes you want to dance, right there and then, which is the only way to dance a Cuban *mambo*—in the middle of a Cuban street, on the Cuban side of Banes.

Almost all of the Americans who live in Banes at the beginning of 1959 are leaving. By the time I am born, American-owned companies like the telephone company and the railways have been confiscated by the revolutionary government, as have the foreign-owned sugar plantations and the sugar mills, like those owned by *La Compañía*. Then Fidel starts taking over the large sugar plantations owned not by rich Americans but by rich Cubans, like the plantation that is owned by his own family, which upsets his mother Lina no end; or the plantation that is managed by my grandfather, my father's father, an old *gallego* I will never meet, who arrived in Cuba with nothing and then slowly built up his family and his home and did well enough to buy a house in the bigger city of Holguin and to send his children to school.

When Fidel takes over the large land-holdings, the Americans in Banes pack up their bags and leave. My mother's aunts tell me later that it was a very sad time because while some Americans were too shy to mix much with Cubans, or at least the Cubans on the Cuban side of town, others were well known and well liked, and they cried when they had to leave Banes, the American part of quiet, prosperous, tropical Banes, and return home to Florida or Georgia or South Carolina, or wherever it is the United Fruit Company sent them to next. I can tell that the version of Banes' history as told by my mother's aunts is a nostalgic and golden retelling, embroidered by old women who may or may not be close to senility. I can also tell, even at my age, that this is a very subversive version of the history of Banes, especially the bits about the United Fruit Company, because this version of history is very different to the version I hear at school.

In the revolutionary version, which is the only version of history we get taught at school, the Spaniards arrived in the area and proceeded to wipe out the native population through maltreatment and disease. In the official version, during the Cuban War of Independence from Spain, the residents of Banes and the surrounding districts were caught in the middle of some quite ferocious battles between the colonial army and the heroic Cuban rebels, Cuban rebels always being heroic. And the eventual arrival of the United Fruit Company was bad news for Banes. The locals had no choice but to work and live in a company town where the Americans and the upper crust of Banes society—who mostly worked for *La Compañía*—led charmed lives in big, rambling timber houses in protected neighbourhoods complete with green lawns, exclusive country clubs and private beaches. Ordinary Cubans were not welcomed, except as domestic help. Meanwhile, the bulk of the population—the poor Cubans—had to work hard to make ends meet cutting sugarcane during harvesting time, but then going hungry for the rest of the year, unless they had a job as a servant to the rich Americans. And when Cubans became too rebellious, the Americans went and brought cheap labour over from the islands near Cuba, from Haiti and Jamaica, which explains why sometimes in Banes, if you pay close attention, you can hear groups of black women standing on a corner talking about God knows what in a strange language, which is probably a version of French or even a version of English, but one that seems foreign to me.

I can tell that the revolutionary version of the history of Banes—in which the poor Cubans are heroes and the rich Americans are not—is a lot more exciting than the version I hear from my mother's aunts, and not just because these old women tend to lose track of what they are saying. In the years to come, I will sit at school listening to my teachers tell us how lucky we are to live here in Banes, to live here in Cuba, because now, Fidel has sent the United Fruit Company and its wealthy, rapacious owners back to the United States, the sugarcane plantations have been 'nationalised', the sugar mills have had their names changed from Preston and Boston to Guatemala and Nicaragua and they now refine and ship Cuban sugar—the best in the world, says my father—to our new communist friends in Eastern Europe, countries with strange-sounding names and exotic histories that are always referred to in the newspaper as 'fraternal' and 'peace-loving'. And the big houses where the Americans and their Cuban lackeys used to live now belong to the People, and the private clubs and the private beaches are open to all Cubans, regardless of whether they are rich or poor, black or white, without them having to ask permission from their American masters.

That much I have been told.

3 · ¡VIVA CUBA SOCIALISTA!

Just sixteen months after my birth, my parents go back to hospital and leave me at home with my mother's best friend, Aunt Hilda. A few days later they come back home bringing with them their new baby. Another boy, whom they name José Antonio and who is supposed to be the spitting image of my father. My parents are over the moon with their new, enlarged family, but it doesn't last long—within three months, they leave home again. My brother is seriously sick. So sick, they need to rush him by ambulance to Holguin, a bigger city a couple of hours away with a much larger and better equipped hospital.

A very sick boy, everyone says when they talk about my baby brother, shaking their heads at the unfairness of it all, and while I am far too young to understand what's going on, when I ask about it years later it becomes painfully clear that these are the hardest days my mother and my father have had to endure—not knowing, my mother tells me, whether her second-born would make it through those first few difficult months. Your brother, he was this close to death, my mother says, and she brings her index finger and her thumb really close together so that there is just a very thin space in between. This close, she says, which is very close.

They are long, long days, with my mother spending almost all her time at the hospital, sitting there by the tiny cot where my brother labours to breathe, hoping that all will be well. My aunt Mirta, who is my mother's youngest sister, is there too, and the rest of the family come and go. My uncle Hector, one of my father's brothers, lives in Holguin and he agrees to give blood any time of the day or night so my brother can live, at least for a little longer. It's day to day. In the meantime I am in Banes, staying now with my father's only sister, my aunt Ana. It will be days before I see my parents again, but when they come back to Banes to check how things are going at the shop, everyone can tell they are totally exhausted, all the stuffing knocked out of them, all their optimism gone, and at night they go to bed without saying much. In the dark, inside his head, I can imagine my father doing something he rarely does—praying. He is pleading with God, the God he rarely talks to, to let his baby son live. He is promising the Virgen de la Caridad del Cobre to do good, to work harder, not to drink another drop of alcohol, ever, to do whatever it takes, to promise whatever needs to be promised, in exchange for God showing just the tiniest bit of mercy and not taking away his baby.

I don't know how many nights my father prayed to the God he doesn't believe in all that much, but the same God was probably listening because eventually, after more than two months, my parents are back in Banes, carrying their baby boy. He is still weak and very skinny and very pale and not totally out of trouble, but alive and getting bigger and a little stronger every day, and it could be because my father talked to God, or it could be because that is what fate had decided for him from the very beginning anyway, or it could be that the doctors in Holguin are really good.

While my parents have been busy doing whatever it takes to keep my baby brother alive, the rest of Banes and the rest of Cuba have been changing faster than anyone would have imagined in January 1959, so fast that some people right here in Banes are not too sure what it all means and decide that it might just be a good time to pack up their bags and spend some time in Miami until things become clear—*hasta que las cosas se aclaren*—which probably means until someone gets rid of Fidel. Because all of a sudden, Cuba has turned away from the United States, the country that has been both its closest neighbour and its interfering protector, and embraced powerful new friends from the other side of the world: the Russians.

If I were older I would understand exactly what's going on. I'd understand why every time you turn on the television, there is a Russian arriving in Havana. You can see it in the old newsreels: Fidel, wearing his olive green uniform and his beard, towering over a funny-looking little man with a trimmed moustache whose name is Anastas Mikoyan. And Mikoyan, who is supposed to be a powerful man in Moscow, hugs Fidel and then tries to give him a kiss—that's right, he tries to give Fidel a kiss, which may be all right in Russia but is not a very Cuban thing to do, everyone says. And on another day, also on the television, there is Fidel wearing a funny fur hat and hugging (but not kissing) Nikita Khrushchev, and shaking hands with Yuri Gagarin, who is Russian and handsome and has blonde hair and blue eyes, unlike most Cubans, and who is the first man to travel into space.

I am too young to understand what has been going on but Cuba has now become the epicentre of the Cold War. Even here in Banes, the Americans who have lived here for so many years have left, and no one is supposed to miss them at all because now

Cuba and the United States no longer talk to each other. The large American companies that used to do a lot of business in Cuba, like the banks and the mining companies and even the United Fruit Company, have all been taken over by the Revolution— they belong to the People now. The Americans, who are not very happy about this, have decided to stop buying Cuban sugar and when Fidel tells them he doesn't care, they decide to break off diplomatic relations with Cuba.

It isn't long before the shortages start, which means the shops are now half empty and you have to queue to buy food or a shirt or a pair of trousers. There are queues even outside my parents' shop, which is a novelty at first. And before you know it, Fidel announces that rationing will be introduced in Cuba, but only for a year, he says, blaming the Americans for this although at the same time he says we don't need the Americans any more because now we have good friends in Moscow who will buy all of our precious sugar at very, very favourable prices. He is speaking in front of what looks like a million people in the big square in Havana that is now known as the Plaza de la Revolución. Standing behind a lectern that is covered with microphones, waving his arms about, pointing his right index finger in defiance at the sky, Fidel says there will be no bourgeois elections in Cuba any more because in Cuba we now have true democracy. We have a socialist Revolution, which makes the crowd go wild applauding and chanting and yelling out, Fidel!, Fidel!, Fidel! Long live socialism, everyone is yelling: ¡Viva Cuba Socialista!

Back home in Banes my mother doesn't understand what it all means, this socialism everyone is talking about. My father does: he says we are becoming a communist country, which is not good at all. He says he has read plenty of stuff about communism and how the Russians invaded Hungary only a few years ago and how in Eastern Europe you always have to queue for food. Besides, the Americans will not be happy to have communism on their doorstep, my father says. He can tell there will be trouble ahead.

★

General Marrero Street stretches from one end of Banes to the other, starting near the river and crossing the bridge that takes you to what used to be the American side of town. It's the street where all the main shops are, including my parents' haberdashery. It's not a big shop, but it's always done well, my mother says. Now, three years after *el Triunfo*, the shelves are looking empty and people aren't coming in as often as they did because there is nothing much to buy. Everything is in short supply. My father says it's because the Americans left and we don't talk to them any more, and our best new friends, the Russians, well, they may have sent that Yuri Gagarin into space and they may be paying lots of money for Cuban sugar and sending their technicians to Havana to help out, but they know nothing about shops.

It's not just my parents' shop that is looking deserted. A couple of doors down from the shop there is a bank. My father says this used to be a very busy bank, but now there is not much point in banking because the new Cuban *pesos* the Revolution has exchanged for the old capitalist *pesos* are not worth much. You can't change them for American dollars, which are now illegal anyway, although I know that my parents keep American dollars hidden in a small cigar box at home. Like everyone else in Banes, except no one ever talks about it. Even if you have one hundred of the revolutionary *pesos* you still won't be able to buy much because there is nothing to spend the money on. But the bank down the road is still open and I can see people coming in and out and I wonder, if my father is right, what those people are doing.

A few doors further down on the other side of my parents' shop is the pharmacy owned by my father's best friend, Enriquito Martínez and his wife Armentina, who is close to my mother. I should say that *used* to be owned by Enriquito because the pharmacy now belongs to the People since Enriquito and his entire family packed up and left for Miami. At home, where no one else can hear, my father keeps talking about just how clever Enriquito was. He was one of the first to see right through the *barbudos*, my father says. He knew pretty early on that Fidel was a communist, despite the endless denials, he says. I think my father misses Enriquito and my mother misses Armentina because they keep talking about them all the time, telling stories of just how much fun they used to have when they were young.

Near the pharmacy is another shop that now belongs to the People: a branch of the department store chain El Encanto, which my mother says used to be the most expensive and best stocked in all of Banes, with the finest clothes, the latest electrical goods from *El Norte*, as everyone calls the United States, and the most delicate fabrics. *Pero eso sí, para la gente que podía.* It was really for the rich. Even today, when its shelves are depleted, the place looks forbiddingly luxurious—the glass and chrome cabinets still sparkle, the lights shine and the black and white tiles on the floor are so polished you can see your reflection bounce back.

Now that we are no longer capitalists but socialists, like they say on the radio, the Revolution has started to take over all the big shops, like El Encanto, on the orders of Fidel, who said on television that in Cuba the exploitation of the masses is over, which means that all the big stores that were owned by rich Cubans now belong to the People. My parents aren't too worried about this because their shop is only a small shop and they can no longer afford to employ anyone because there is nothing much to sell in the shop and not too many customers, not even the *guajiros* who used to come and buy all their clothes on credit.

Still, the Revolution is working in very strange ways because one morning my father arrives at the *Retacería García* to find two *milicianos* waiting. They have guns and they look very serious as they tell my father that his shop is under investigation because he exploits workers and, *compañero* (which is what everyone now calls everyone else in socialist Cuba), you must hand over your keys and go home while we check what's going on. And my father, who recounts the story in tones that could probably be described as a mixture of anger and panic, doesn't want to give them the keys but he does in the end because they carry guns and he thinks there is not much point refusing.

For the next few days my parents wait at home, not knowing what is going on at the shop. They go to the only lawyer they know in Banes, but the lawyer shakes his head and says there is not much he can do either. There is not much anyone can do, he adds. They talk to my aunt Mirta, who knows a lot more about business than they do, but she doesn't know what's going on either. My mother even talks to my uncle Papi, who is now really involved in the Revolution, but there is nothing he can do. Just wait, everyone says. Wait. But my father doesn't want to wait and someone suggests that perhaps, just perhaps, his mother, my grandmother Fulgencia, may be able to do something.

My grandmother, a formidable Spaniard, is a close friend of another formidable Spaniard in the district who happens to be the mother of a man called Sergio del Valle. And Sergio del Valle is not just any Sergio del Valle, but a *barbudo* who is now a high ranking member of the Revolutionary Government and who is close to Fidel, and because this is Cuba, everyone knows for sure that while Sergio may be very busy helping Fidel with the Revolution and everything, he will still have time to listen to his mother. So my grandmother talks to Sergio's mother and Sergio's mother probably rings Sergio in his Havana office and has a talk to him about my parents' shop and probably tells him, too, before she hangs up, to eat, because he looks so skinny on television, and then, next thing we know, the *milicianos* who asked my father for the keys knock on the door at home and hand the keys back to my father, who is beside himself with relief. So is my mother, who says, *Gracias a Dios, Gracias a Dios,* thinking that God—who else?—has given her back her shop, when in fact she should be thanking my grandmother Fulgencia and my grandmother's friend, Sergio's mother.

4 · MISSILES IN PARADISE

My mother says we are off to the beach. On doctor's orders. My brother has been so ill for so long that the doctor has recommended, with typically Cuban certainty, that what my brother needs—what we all need—is to spend some time by the seaside, taking in the fresh air and enjoying the hot, Caribbean sun. So, we are off to the beach. To Playa de Morales, which is only about fourteen kilometres away from Banes but seems much further.

One of my father's friends who used to be well off before the Revolution—*estaba muy bien*, is how my father puts it—but who is now in the same situation as everybody else, has lent his Morales beach house to my father for three months. It's not a flash house. It's a timber house with a very basic kitchen, very basic furniture and an outside latrine. There is no electricity in Morales, so we make do with a couple of large Chinese-made kerosene lamps and some candles. It's a little more primitive than what we are used to at home in Banes, but the house is right on the beach, in a fairly isolated part of Morales, and the sun shines

27

every morning when we wake up, and the water is always blue and clear and magically warm.

There is a house next door, owned by another friend of my father's, Felelo and his family, and they have a boy about my age who becomes my instant best friend. But apart from us and Felelo and his family there is almost no one here, and we can sit outside by the water and look into the horizon and see nothing much most days. We know that if you keep swimming into that horizon, sooner or later you will get to *El Norte*, assuming that neither the sharks nor the Cuban *milicianos* get you first. But for the moment, no one is thinking of leaving Cuba.

Sure, things are getting tougher. It's true that since last year when those Yankee-backed invaders failed in their attempt to land at the Bay of Pigs—which in revolutionary Cuba is called by the much more heroic name of Playa de Girón—the Revolutionary Government has become even less tolerant of anyone who may have fancy ideas about elections. Nowadays, you watch what you say, which means it's almost always better not to say anything that might be misunderstood by your family or your neighbours as being somehow against the Revolution, let alone critical of *El Maxímo Líder.* But right now, all this business is far, far away from our little paradise here in Morales. Or so we think.

Every morning my father leaves for Banes, catching a ride with our neighbour, so he can open up the shop. Then, in the afternoon, he comes back from work. It only takes him about half an hour because it isn't that far and because the number of privately owned cars on the road is rapidly diminishing. There is no petrol around and no spare parts from the United States to keep the cars going the way they are supposed to. Instead, the roads are full of military trucks and jeeps, always rushing somewhere in the service of the People. While my father is away, my brother and I play on the white sand with our neighbour's son and occasionally with some other kids our age whose fathers seem to be *milicianos* keeping an eye along the coastline. It's paradise and from what my mother says, it's doing a world of wonders for my brother's health.

Finding food is a problem, but then again, this is always a problem in Cuba now. My father brings food from Banes, whatever he can find, and there is always someone coming around offering to sell something, or to exchange it for something else. But this is done on the quiet because, as we all know, there is no such thing as a black market in Cuba. Yet when you least expect it, someone knocks on your door, trying to exchange some plantains for a pair of trousers. Pork meat is a problem, though. Cubans love pork. It's the national dish, which may be why it is strictly controlled by the government. The theory is that no one in egalitarian, socialist Cuba should eat more pork than their neighbours, so the government controls supply and demand. It means you have to be careful when someone knocks on your door and offers to sell you a chunk of pork, because if you get caught selling or buying meat on the black market—if you get caught in possession of half a cow, say, or with half a well-fed pig in the boot of your car—you are in big, big trouble. You can go to prison. I know this—every child in Cuba knows this. You get caught with meat, you can kiss your family goodbye and go straight to prison.

Today someone knocked on the door at Morales and offered to sell us pork. And not just anyone, but a *miliciano* who lives near Morales and is supposed to be one of the big military bosses in this area. My father knows him well enough to invite him in but not well enough to trust him when the *miliciano* says he has some pork left over and is happy to sell it. It's quite an offer. Meat! Tempting, but in the end caution wins the day and my father tells him, *Muchas gracias, compañero, pero no necesitamos carne.* Thanks but no, we do not need any meat, he lies. In Cuba, he says later, when the *miliciano* leaves, it pays to be careful. My mother nods in agreement.

Now, at night, my father is sitting on the narrow veranda at the front of the house, facing the beach, which is all dark, though you can hear the slow rhythm of the tropical waves, a sound that makes me want to go to sleep right there and then. My father sits there smoking one of his cigars, as he always does at night after dinner, and talking to our neighbour Felelo. My father says, You won't believe what happened today—that *miliciano* from up the road came to sell us meat. Can you believe that?

Felelo says, Did you buy any?

My father says, You've got to be joking. You think I am stupid? I knew it was a trap . . .

No, *chico*, no, says Felelo, sounding incredulous. You turned down meat? Pork? *Estas loco* . . . You are crazy, man. It's okay. I buy meat from him all the time. He is a communist but he is all right.

And that is how Cuba is divided now—there are the communists, and there are the communists who are all right. The ones who are all right are the ones whose job it is to protect the Revolution from the Americans, but who also come knocking on your door offering to sell you contraband pork.

I know my father could kick himself because, let's face it, a nice bit of *lechón*, at the beach, with a cold beer, well, is there anything more Cuban than that? Everyone is quiet on the veranda and you can tell they are all thinking about the pork and hoping against hope that, having been politely but revolutionarily turned away by my suspicious father, the *miliciano* will nevertheless come back at some stage in the next few days, offering to sell us more pork. Still, there is a light breeze and the stars are out, as they are every night in Cuba, and soon enough everyone has forgotten about the pork and gone back to arguing about something else, like the baseball. It's paradise.

I don't know this now but within days, paradise will be no more. One night my father arrives home from Banes pretty excited. The Americans, he says, are ready to invade Cuba. It's everywhere on the television, in the paper and on the radio—Fidel says he knows for sure that the Yankee imperialists are readying to invade Cuba, and that brave, revolutionary Cubans will fight to the last drop of blood to defend their country. My mother looks out to sea to see if she can spot the American invaders, but there is nothing on the horizon. Some days later, everything becomes clearer—the Americans have gone to the United Nations and said that the Soviet Union, our new best friends, are building missile bases in Cuba, just one hundred miles from the United States. Missiles? In Cuba? Incredible.

True or not, my mother has gone into panic mode. She is sure the Americans will invade and she is sure that this means bad news for everyone because there will be war, she knows it, and she hates war, and she worries about my father being called up and her brothers, too, to fight the Americans. And this time, she says, the Americans won't send exiled Cubans like they did at the Bay of Pigs last year, no sir, this time they will send real American fighters with big guns, and there will be much blood shed. So in her own way she starts getting ready for war, putting away tins of Romanian processed meat (the type she tries to disguise with some garlic and a bit of cumin, if she can find some somewhere) and some black beans and a few candles. It's not enough to feed the family for a couple of days, let alone a couple of weeks, but that's all there is.

Days later again, my father arrives with big news from Banes: an American spy plane has been shot down right in the middle of town. Well, on the outskirts, really, but everyone in

Banes swears it's right in the middle of town. It was a U2, an American spy plane with powerful cameras that allow the pilot to take photographs so precise, my father has been told, they can see all the way over in Washington whether you have hung out the washing that morning. Now we all know things are getting serious. As my father tells it, every morning for weeks, while my mother and my brother and I have been enjoying the beach, Banes has been buzzed by American U2 planes, flying really close to the houses, up and down the area, presumably taking pictures of people's washing. No one knew what it was all about but now, my father says, everyone has put two and two together and believe that the pictures the American planes have taken are of some of the missiles being installed right here in Banes!

Which may explain the Russian technicians who appear to have materialised in town in the past months, according to my father. With short-cropped hair, pink skin and a liking for bright, tropical prints that most Cubans would find in appallingly bad taste, the visitors don't mix much, probably because they don't speak or understand Spanish. Our Russian comrades, as they are called on the radio, are everywhere and nowhere. They seem to disappear during the day. Now, it all makes sense. My father says the place where some of the missiles have been photographed is in Los Angeles, a desolate area just a few kilometres out of Banes. The Americans, as usual, seem to know everything that is going on in Cuba.

But today, the Americans have paid a price for knowing too much: the Cuban anti-aircraft guns that have been stationed just outside Banes for months have shot down an American plane creating, says my father, quite a commotion. ¡Tremendo! he says. Like everyone else, he first heard the buzzing plane really close to the shop rooftops, then the distant gunfire, and then he watched as the plane came down and he closed the shop and, like everyone else, rushed on foot to see what had happened and whether this was, after all, the much-heralded invasion by the Americans which, he secretly hoped in his heart, would solve everything. In truth, my father will admit many years later, he didn't get to see all that much because by the time half the town arrived to witness this piece of Cold War history—the only instance of combat during the confrontation that would become known as the Cuban Missile Crisis—Cuban *milicianos* and the Soviet technicians with their loud shirts and short-cropped military hairstyles had cordoned off much of the area, to keep curious onlookers away.

But my father still knows a lot about what happened, he is telling us excitedly, because one of his friends, Juanito, was one of the first to be taken to the scene by the *milicianos*. Everyone in Banes knows that Juanito is an expert when it comes to cameras, so they took him to where the plane was shot down to inspect the cameras attached to the aircraft. Juanito told my father that he didn't recognise the cameras on the plane but that he did get a good look at the dead pilot, who must have died on impact—he was sure of this. And all the pilot had on him was a revolver, a US$5 note and a funny-looking small paper sachet of powder which my father thinks must have been stock, the type you mix with hot water to make instant soup, but which Juanito swears, on his mother's grave, was some sort of spying gadget.

We listen to the story in disbelief, except for my mother, who thinks the world is about to end and that we are going to get caught in the middle of a war with the Americans, stuck in this remote beach house, cut off from what is going on in the rest of the country, and away from her beloved family. My father tries to reassure her and so, later on, do our neighbours. Everything will be all right. But everything is not all right. The

Cuban Missile Crisis is raging around us as my brother and I swim in the tropical waters and play on the white sands, building castles and roads and pretending that the rocks we are using as cars are really big military trucks carrying missiles and guns to protect the Revolution. As the crisis escalates, it becomes quite clear that my mother is right, at least about us being stuck in Morales. My father arrives home one afternoon with news that all the roads around Banes have been closed off by the military, including the only road in and out of Morales. He has locked up the shop in Banes for good, and from now on we are staying put here, waiting anxiously to see what happens.

By now, Morales has become a military camp of sorts. The beachfront has been taken over by *milicianos* in their trucks and jeeps, and we have been told to stay in the house or just inside the front, which means we can't go exploring in the bush or along the beach without my mother rushing out and yelling at us to get back in here, do you want to get killed and give me a heart attack? When my mother looks up at the horizon, she can see the ships. There are five, six, probably a dozen huge, grey American ships anchored just off the coast. The ships look really close, as if you could almost swim to them, and they look threatening, making my mother even more nervous than she already is, which is plenty. At least one of the American ships is an aircraft carrier because from the shore, you can see planes take off, flying over the other ships and then disappearing out to sea until they look like tiny dots in the blue sky.

Over the next couple of days we have no idea what's going on, since my father cannot go to Banes and bring us fresh news. All we know is that we have been told to stay put. And then, in the middle of what historians will later describe as the closest and most dangerous encounter of the Cold War, just as my mother's carefully rationed kitty is starting to run out, our old *miliciano* friend comes back knocking on the door, offering us some pork. It's a miracle, says my mother, who is really not very religious but can tell a miracle when she sees one. This time there is no hesitation on my parents' part. They buy the pork, thinking that if we are soon going to be at war with the Americans, then we might as well have some pork for dinner.

Maybe it was something to do with the pork, but now we have another visitor. My aunt Mirta arrives from her home in the nearby town of San Germán, where she and her husband have what was, *antes del Triunfo*, a large and growing department store. My aunt, like the rest of the family, has been frantic, having had no news from us for days. Like everyone else, the rest of the family expects the Americans to invade and fight the Russians on the island, a prospect that fills almost all with absolute dread. So, my aunt says, speaking really quickly like Cubans do when they are excited, she has been doing all she can to try and get to Morales and bring us back to Banes, so that if there is an invasion, well, at least we will all be close by.

Somehow, my aunt has managed to borrow a car in San Germán, get some rationed petrol and drive straight to Morales where she has done the impossible and broken through the military cordon that surrounds the area. If anyone in our family could do it, it is my aunt Mirta. As my mother says, she could sell refrigerators in the Arctic. And now, here she is on our doorstep in one of her colourful dresses and her American-style sunglasses, and everyone is hugging as if we haven't seen each other for years, and talking at the same time and asking what the hell is going on and is Fidel still in Havana? My mother packs as quickly as she can, throwing our belongings into suitcases and bags and working on the not-too-fanciful notion that at some stage, somewhere, a *miliciano* will appear and take my crazy aunt and everyone else to prison for disobeying orders. We jump in the car and drive out to the road that will, all things being equal, take us back home.

It's only when we hit the first of several military roadblocks that my mother admits to having packed up the leftover pork. She doesn't tell anyone, but in her mind, she admits later, she can imagine the *milicianos* stopping the car, inspecting the boot and finding the two or three kilos of contraband pork, a counter-revolutionary act so perverse, so anti-socialist, that she and her entire family will be banished forever to some prison at the other end of the island. And yet it seems the option of stopping the car somewhere out of sight, opening the boot and throwing away the incriminating pork is not considered seriously either by my parents or by my aunt Mirta, confirming yet again that when it comes to the country of my birth, it's folly to stand between a Cuban and a pork cutlet.

God probably understands all about pork cutlets, though, because somehow my aunt Mirta manages, with some help from my father, to assure the *milicianos* along the way that we are, indeed, a family that got stuck in Morales and just wants to go home and help defend the Revolution, like Fidel says. Until we arrive at the last checkpoint, at the very entrance to Banes, where we are promptly taken into custody and told to drive to the local police station, presumably to explain what we are doing in a private car, driving around the country when the Americans are just a few miles away in their big ships, waiting to land. No one can hear it, but my poor mother's heart is racing at a hundred miles an hour, for sure.

Still, God probably *does* understand all about pork cutlets because the *milicianos* who have taken us to the police station haven't searched the car yet and as we enter the station my father immediately recognises one of his friends behind the station counter. His name is Hugo and he just happens to be in charge today and he asks my father what is going on. We explain and Hugo tells my father, *Mi socio*, don't worry about it, go home and make sure the family is looked after. I will sort this out. My father will be forever grateful.

Years later, trying to recall the details of those momentous days back in October 1962 when the world came close to nuclear war, I ask my mother what she was thinking when she wrapped up the pork and dumped it in the boot of the car. What was I thinking? she says incredulously. We had pork, she says, emphasising the word. What were we supposed to do? Leave behind good Cuban pork? *Que va.* No way, you never leave good Cuban pork behind!

5 · GOOD LITTLE COMMUNISTS

As I walk into the classroom for my first day at the Jose Antonio Saco primary school, I am welcomed by my teacher, Flor, who will in fact be my teacher throughout my primary school years. Like all good teachers, she will teach and nurture me and decades later she will still be remembered fondly. Even her name—which translates as Flower—makes an immediate impact on an impressionable child.

Flor is short, her skin is the colour of creamy milk chocolate, she is softly spoken, and she wears small metal-rimmed glasses that give her an air of absolute mastery in all things scholastic. But I still don't want to be here. I hate it. I want to be home, with my younger brother, playing out in the street with my friends as we normally do, or mucking about at my parents' shop, running around and knocking over rolls of material and giving my mother an almighty headache. No amount of begging, no amount of crying and negotiating, has convinced my father to let me stay at home or in the shop. Trying to convince my mother, always the soft touch, has been useless, although she promises to come and pick me up at midday to take me home for lunch. Instead, here I am, sitting down at the desk that has been allocated to me by the teacher, thinking of escape.

The school is on the same street as my parents' shop, just a block or so away, but I know that's not the place to escape to because that is where my father is, behind the counter, and I am sure he won't be happy to see me. So I wait in class until recess and then, without looking back, I walk out of the classroom, down the stairs and across the steaming hot cement playground, through the big iron gates and then I run to the corner, cross the main street and, as fast as I can, rush across two more streets without looking back, no way, until I get home. Even at this age I can see this is quite a feat but it is one that is not about to be rewarded because for some reason both my father and my mother are at home. And they are not happy. Only my younger brother is happy to see me—and he doesn't count. My mother, like all good Cuban mothers, rushes to me and hugs me and asks what I am doing home, and why I am sweating and did I really cross those dangerous streets on my own? *Dios mio, ¡este niño!* My father explodes, takes me by the arms, smacks me across the legs hard enough to make me cry and, despite my mother's protestations, drags me, still sobbing, out of the house, across the streets I have just traversed and back through the gates of the school.

I am screaming now, not just because my father's grip on my arm hurts but because I know full well I am defeated. He drags me up the stairs and into the classroom where every pair of eyes fixes on the loud kid who keeps screaming that he wants his mum, that he wants to go home. My father, who is livid with anger, picks me up in the air and then drops me onto the chair behind the desk with enough force to shake the seat, and then looks me straight in the eye and says, Don't you dare move from that desk. I am petrified, but from the corner of my eye I can see her, I can see Flor, my teacher, my saviour, coming towards us, and then as she gets to me she hugs me and she looks at my father and says something like, I am sure he is not going anywhere, Luis . . . I am sure, and she keeps hugging me until my father walks out. And eventually I stop crying.

It doesn't take me long to discover that despite my initial reservations, I am going to enjoy school after all. We sit at our uncomfortable wooden desks learning to recite an alphabet where the F is for Fidel, the R for rifle and the Y for Yankees. Learning about Fidel and rifles and why we should hate the Americans can sometimes take up a fair amount of the school day, even in primary school. As we get older, more and more time is taken out for what my parents describe with growing alarm as indoctrination. At this stage I don't know what they are talking about—I just think they get alarmed about everything.

Some days we attend commemorations held outside the Communist Party headquarters, a big old house right in the main street. Until a couple of years ago the house belonged to the Gonzalez family, regular friends of my parents who were well known all over Banes. When they left for the United States the house and everything in it was taken over by the People, like all the other houses vacated by *gusanos*, and who could be more representative of the People than the Communist Party? That is why they have made the house the headquarters of the Party in Banes. *La Casa del Partido*, as everyone calls it, is just a couple of doors down from my school so it's easy for us to march in near perfect unison from the playground up the street to attend protest meetings or to commemorate some revolutionary anniversary, or to swear loyalty to the Revolution: *Patria o Muerte. ¡Venceremos!* Fatherland or Death. We shall win! Which is how all speeches end in Cuba now.

Attending these *actos revolucionarios*, as they are called, means we get to stand in the sun listening to speeches until one of the older students is asked to step forward and, with great ceremony, raise the Cuban flag while we sing the national anthem and the 'Internationale', which is the best part of the whole thing, not only because I enjoy singing the 'Internationale' but because it means the ceremony is over and we get to move into the shade and sometimes they bring out orange flavoured soft drinks in small glass bottles with the name Coca-Cola etched on the glass. When I ask my mother, she tells me Coca-Cola is the name of an American soft drink from *antes del Triunfo*. Now, she says, the factory that used to make it is owned by the Revolutionary Government. It still makes soft drinks and uses the same bottles but they don't call it Coca-Cola any more.

The speeches that come before we get the soft drinks are long and they make you want to be anywhere else rather than standing in the sun, sweating in your uniform and getting thirstier and thirstier. But my friends and I still enjoy these *actos revolucionarios* because it means missing mathematics, which I hate anyway, or science, and all this talk about revolutionary heroes, about Lenin and Marx, makes us feel very grown up. It makes us feel like good communists, just as Fidel says we should. We like the marching, and the fact that we get shown how to assemble and reassemble Russian machine guns and that we get to salute the flag and swear to give our lives, if necessary, on behalf of the Revolution. Why not? As Fidel always says, the fact that we can go to school and read and write, regardless of how rich or poor our families are, is all due to the Revolution. One of my friends says reading and writing were invented by the Revolution, which I know is not true.

I am not sure, however, whether my teacher Flor is all that keen on this revolutionary stuff. She looks thoroughly bored by the whole thing, and I wonder whether she may be . . . you know, a *gusano* after all. My parents aren't too keen on this revolutionary stuff either, which is bad news for me because there is nothing I want more right now, after the *acto revolucionario* is finished and I return to class, than to put my hand up and ask Flor if I can become a Communist Pioneer—a *pionero*—which is what all good revolutionary children want to become. When you become a *pionero* you get to go on excursions, give speeches at important events and wear a blue and white *pañueleta* scarf around your neck to show the world you are proud to be a good little communist. You also get to go on trips to other towns and to the beach, and sometimes they teach you how to fire a rifle, shooting in the distance at cardboard figures that are always dressed like bloodthirsty American soldiers who want to destroy the Revolution. If you are a really good *pionero*, you even get to meet visiting Communist Pioneers from the Soviet Union, and if you are a really, really good revolutionary pioneer you may even get to visit Russia or one of the fraternal countries in Eastern Europe, and there is no bigger prize in Cuba than getting a trip overseas, anywhere overseas, even if it is to the Soviet Union. Or Romania.

But despite all this, my parents refuse to let me join the *pioneros*. They say it's just a way of indoctrinating children. It's a problem, though, because many of my friends are proud *pioneros* and I am not, which can only mean one thing: my parents are not good revolutionaries. They are suspect. They may even be *gusanos*. And I am scared they may get into trouble, that the police will come home, or worse, that the woman who runs the Committee for the Defence of the Revolution in our neighbourhood will knock on the door and ask my father why he never puts his name down for voluntary work, why he doesn't attend political meetings, why there is no picture of Fidel anywhere in our house.

Can you explain, *compañero*, why your son is not a *pionero*? And so one day I arrive home wearing my scarf, beaming proudly, because not only have I become a good revolutionary but now my parents are safe, and no one is going to come and question them.

My excitement doesn't last long. My father looks at me in disbelief and asks, with not even a hint of humour, what am I wearing around my neck. A *pionero* scarf, I reply, sensing this is not working out the way I expected. Well, he says, you can take it off right now and tomorrow morning, first thing you do when you get to school is you go to your teacher and give the *pañueleta* back. No son of mine is going to be a communist.

Next morning I do as I am told, and as I explain to my teacher that my father has asked me to return the *pañueleta*, I imagine that our whole world is about to collapse around us, that we are doomed, because we are all suspect.

★

It's cyclone season in Cuba so everyone has been waiting anxiously to see whether one will develop and, if it does, just where and how quickly it will come through Banes. My father says we go through this every year but most of the time nothing much happens, except for some heavy rain and wind. Then it's back to normal.

This time, however, a real cyclone is definitely coming. My father has no doubt about it and neither, it seems, does anyone else. Everyone has been getting ready for the past day or so, listening to the radio and television for weather updates. Even Fidel has made an appearance, interrupting some program or other as he always does, so he can speak for three hours on why everyone should be prepared for the cyclone and explaining, in detail, the best way to put tape on the windowpanes to make sure they are not shattered by the heavy winds that are making their way up and around the Gulf of Mexico.

While my father is busy trying to secure the windows from outside the house, my mother is in full panic mode. She has seen many cyclones, she says, and she knows what it means. Like everyone else in Cuba, she can remember the last big cyclone, Cyclone Flora, which razed much of the island in 1963, resulting in 1150 deaths that made news for weeks. And she fears this one is going to be as bad as Flora. She thinks all cyclones are as bad as Flora. So, don't tell her about cyclones and don't tell her about not needing to panic, and don't tell her about how it will all be okay because she *knows* what a cyclone can do.

It's been decided that we are going to the family house on Presidente Zayas Avenue because that house is bigger and stronger than where we live and it is also in a higher area of otherwise dead-flat Banes. My mother runs around packing clothes for my brother and me and raiding the kitchen cabinets looking for whatever is there that can be taken with us. My father will stay behind to finish securing our house and then he will go to the shop to close up while my brother, my mother and I are on our way across town to the house where my mother grew up. I don't mind at all because some of my other cousins will also be there, and the whole thing, I think, is going to be a bit of a party, like most things Cubans do. I know my mother is very scared because I can hear it in her voice but I am sure that once we are all at the house and my father has joined us, someone will go into the kitchen and make some Cuban coffee and start cooking something for dinner and then, before you know it, everything will be okay.

Once we get to the house, though, I can see the wind has picked up outside. We are looking out the windows on to the street, and the rain is getting heavier. Water is seeping into the house under the front door. And the wind, which was pretty strong when we made our way across town, is now getting even stronger. I can hear it whistle and crash against the trees and the fence outside, and against the side of the big wooden house, shaking it as if it were made of paper. There isn't going to be a party quite yet.

When my father finally arrives my mother calms down a bit, except now she worries about my uncle Papi and his wife, my aunt Mary, asking why they haven't made their way up the hill yet. We all wait for the worst. The electricity is cut off so we can't even listen to the radio—not that we could have heard much above the noise outside. By the way the house is shuddering, I figure the heart of the cyclone isn't too far off, but in fact it takes hours and when it finally arrives in full force we all go quiet because everyone is dead scared. It feels as if the house is about to be torn in half—the walls are shaking, there is water coming in through the ceiling where the sheets of corrugated iron have been twisted at the corners, and the windows are rattling despite the best efforts of my uncles, who have meticulously taped over every bit of exposed glass. When we look out the windows into the backyard, it's like what I imagine one of those big South American rivers look like—the Amazon, say—a torrent of muddy water sweeping away everything in its path.

I look out one of the front windows, across the street to the house on the other side, where the Polish-born Jewish family lives, the ones that, according to one of my cousins, escaped from the Nazis during the Second World War and somehow, I have never asked exactly how, ended up in Cuba. Just to the side and front of their house there is a huge tree that I have been watching for a while because even though it's tall and strong, it is bending from the force of the wind, and losing many of its branches.

45

It's just like watching cartoons at the cinema because the tree bends and then tries to straighten up again and then it bends one more time and again and again until it happens—the tree doesn't straighten again but falls over, almost in slow motion, crashing to the ground and making a noise that sounds like an explosion. It's so loud we can all hear it inside the house above the noise of the rain and the wind.

It takes a few more hours before the wind finally dies down. The rain continues for two or three days, causing even more damage and flooding houses and shops across Banes, but not here where we are, in the highest part of town. There is no electricity but there is a gas stove, so my mother and my aunts start cooking, which is what you do in Cuba when the worst is over. Next morning my father goes home and to the shop and comes back hours later with the news—the house is fine, although there has been some flooding and he will need to repair the roof; and the shop survived, as did most other shops in the street, except for a couple of windows at the back, which allowed some rain to get in.

After three days that seem more like a week, we pack up our things and head back down the little hill to our house and then back to school and back to the queues. On television, there is Fidel again, explaining how the worst is over. He means the cyclone, of course. Everything else is back to normal.

6 · A CARNIVAL AND A FUNERAL

Don't ask me how this came about but my father arrived home to tell us that he has been made the supply chief of the carnival. Talk about a surprise.

Every year, towns and cities up and down the island, no matter how small, how poor or how far from Havana, hold their own street carnival, and Banes is no different. Mind you, the Banes carnival is nowhere near as glamorous or as well known as the Havana carnival, which has a huge parade through the main streets of the capital and is televised across the country; or the carnival in Santiago de Cuba, which everyone says is the original Cuban carnival—and the wildest of them all. Still, for the next two weeks the town goes berserk. It's really the ultimate Cuban party, which means that everyone goes to work or school during the daytime but as soon as the sun sets you come out again, dressed in your Sunday best, to join in the fun. The main streets are closed off to traffic for the duration, and for weeks beforehand dozens of temporary stalls are built along the streets to sell beer, rum and food—and no rationing. It all sounds to me a little too capitalist, but no one is complaining. Even Fidel says Cubans should enjoy the carnival.

Almost every night there is music, too, especially on the Saturday nights, with loudspeakers blaring cha-cha-chas and *rumbas* and *guagancos*, and orchestras and singers from all over Cuba, even from as far as Havana, make their way to Banes so they can play live atop a temporary bandstand set up in the Parque Domínguez, just across from the church. The bandstand is decorated with palm trees, paper garlands and revolutionary slogans encouraging Banes to work harder to make Cuba even more of a socialist paradise, presumably so there is more time for carnival. It's strange to see the slogans up there talking about revolutionary sacrifice while everyone is having a great time down on the dance floor, but that's the way things are in Cuba.

It's even stranger to think that my father, who never puts his name down for voluntary work and who hasn't joined and is unlikely to ever join the Communist Party, or so he says, has been made supply chief of the carnival—the best carnival time job of all, except maybe for being Queen of the Carnival. But that job only goes to pretty teenage girls who are chosen by someone somewhere in the local Communist Party, not just for her beauty but also for her revolutionary fervour. Most of the time, the Queen of the Carnival turns out to be related to someone in the Party but I am sure that is just coincidence. Still, the Queen of the Carnival only gets to swan around town with a cardboard tiara and ride on a truck as part of the procession, which takes place on the first Saturday night of the carnival. On the other hand, my father gets to organise the stalls, organise the supply of food and alcohol, collect and bank all the takings at the end of the day and make sure that everything runs smoothly.

What's more, he gets to meet and take care of all the celebrities who come to town to perform. This year the star attraction, the act everyone in Banes wants to see, is a duo called Clara y Mario. They are both in their late thirties, I think, and they sing sad *boleros* about lovers who love each other too much for their own good. Clara y Mario are glamorous and good-looking in a way that no one in Banes could ever emulate, or at least no one that I know in Banes. They are probably the most popular singing duo in Cuba right now, always performing on television and radio, and having, I am sure, their own fan club. They are the most famous people to come to Banes for a long time, and so everyone is pretty excited about it. And now, my father is going to meet Clara y Mario, believe it or not, and make sure they have everything they need while staying at the Hotel Bani right on General Marrero Street. It is the only hotel in town, a two-storey timber building with a bar downstairs.

My mother and all her friends want to know what Clara y Mario are really like. They want to know if they are married to each other. And how does Clara get her beehive hairstyle to stay up just so when everyone knows you can't buy hairspray anywhere in Cuba any more because the Americans took all the hairspray back home with them? Are they really as glamorous as they look? My father, who is taking his job seriously, is happy to impart the occasional bit of celebrity gossip but then he says he is very busy with all this organising and, really, he has to get back to checking that no one has their fingers in the till and making sure none of the stalls runs out of beer because, well, things can get nasty when you run out of beer right after listening to one of those heartbreaking Clara y Mario *boleros*, you know . . .

For the next two weeks I feel as if I am the most popular kid at school because everyone knows that my father is a big boss at the carnival headquarters, which also means we get to eat nice food at home as he controls all the extra supplies coming in for carnival time, and we get to stock up on beer and the occasional bottle of rum because, after all, that is what is expected when you are a big boss of the carnival. I am proud of my father because I can see he is enjoying the job, too, despite the responsibility and despite the fact that he arrives home in the very early hours of the morning, sometimes at four am, with all this money he has collected from the stalls and for which he has to account, and he sits there making sure the numbers add up and then places the notes neatly in piles which he puts inside empty cigar boxes.

My mother worries about my father coming home so late with all that money because she knows that when carnival comes around, there is always trouble. Although my brother and I get to go out and listen to the music and just walk around the stalls with my mother almost every night, we never get to see the trouble because she makes sure we are home and in bed at a reasonable time. But the next day at school we always hear stories about a man who was drunk and discovered his wife kissing some other man who was also drunk, and then someone produced a big knife and threatened to kill the wife and her lover, and half of Banes as well, but in the end no one got killed because a *miliciano* arrived just in time and fired his revolutionary pistol in the air. And while I am sure that the stories are probably exaggerated and the incidents made out to be much more serious than they really are, I am worried that these stories are not going to impress Clara y Mario very much.

My mother's grandmother has died. She was one hundred and eight, which my aunt Nidia says could have made her the oldest person in Banes, although no one knows for sure. She is not really my grandmother but we still call her *Abuela* because that is what everyone calls her and, besides, I never met my mother's mother, my real *abuela*, who died before I was even born.

Abuela lived with my aunt Nidia in the family home in Presidente Zayas Avenue, where she was always surrounded by noisy relatives and gossiping neighbours; it seems to me having lots of family around you is not the worst way to die, if you have to die. To be honest, I found *Abuela* a little scary. Sitting in her rocking chair on the front veranda, she looked as old and small and wrinkled as you can expect to be when you are one hundred and eight, and because her eyesight wasn't all that good any more she squinted at everyone who arrived as if trying to remember their name or where they were from. She sat there, rocking away for what seemed like hours on end, chewing on her dentures, sometimes singing old Spanish songs I could never understand, and occasionally saying something out of the blue that had my aunt Nidia shaking her head or rolling her eyes, and telling *Abuela* it might be time to have some dinner, or even time to go to bed.

Whenever my brother and I visited, which was two or three times a week, my mother insisted we give *Abuela* a kiss on her cheeks, which was not something I looked forward to. It was like kissing parched paper—rough, wrinkly—and she smelled faintly of stale cologne, and when we kissed her she would say something about how grown up we looked, and then, without fail, she'd stick her dentures out at me, which really, really scared me. I think she did it deliberately too, because she would then give me a little hint of a smile. She is dead now.

When I ask, my mother says *Abuela* died of old age, which seems like a plausible explanation. I can tell that while everyone is sad about *Abuela*'s death, there is also relief. All my aunts and uncles and even the neighbours say the same thing: *Abuela* had a long life, but it was a hard life, a poor woman's life, a life of looking after children and then her grandchildren and even the great grandchildren. Now, they say, she can finally rest in peace.

This is my first funeral. My mother says funerals are not for children because funerals are too sad and they give you nightmares, but she relents and agrees that my brother and I, along with our older cousins, can say farewell to *Abuela* at the funeral parlour, provided we change into what she calls respectable clothes, and provided we behave when we get there, which of course we promise to do without the need for much prompting.

It's quite an event, but then again, Cuban funerals always are. For three nights *Abuela* has been here in the funeral home— which is in the middle of town, as you would expect—in a black, shiny coffin with gold-coloured handles. The coffin is at the end of the long room, at about waist level if you are a grown-up, surrounded by a sea of wreaths which give the room the kind of funny smell that sticks to your clothes for days. They say it's the smell of the flowers, but even I know it's really the smell of death.

My father takes my brother and me closer to the coffin, and then he lifts each of us in turn so we can see inside. When I look in, it seems to me as if *Abuela* is not dead at all but just having a siesta, except her face seems too white and she is not playing around with her dentures. It's still scary and I can now understand what my mother meant about nightmares. As I lean forward to give her a farewell kiss on her cheek, I hang on to my father really tightly because I am afraid of falling right into the coffin, right next to my dead *abuela*. I know for sure I will have nightmares.

As I look around the room, I imagine *Abuela* must have had lots of friends because the room is pretty full. It's peak viewing time, in the early evening, right after dinner, and the women, most of them in respectful black, are sitting around on hard wooden chairs we call *taburetes* gossiping in a way that is supposed to be quiet and private but in reality, this being Cuba, is a little too loud and slightly chaotic, so you can hear exactly what they are saying and about whom.

The men, like my father, pay their respects and then move out to the front veranda or onto the footpath outside, to talk about baseball, or about what's going on in Havana, and smoke their cigars, doing their best to ignore my cousins and me and all the other kids from the neighbourhood who, instead of going to the cinema as they do almost every night, have come to the funeral home on their bikes so we can run around the street, yelling at the top of our lungs and getting our best clothes dirty.

There is no music, but the whole thing is like one big party, with cigars and coffee. The thing about Cuban funerals is that when you turn up, regardless of the time, someone will inevitably make coffee and come around with a big tray loaded with tiny china cups of *café cubano*, so dark and sweet you can feel your teeth crumble when you drink it. Right behind the coffee comes someone offering cigars to the men, who never say no because on Cuba you never say no to a cigar, even if you don't light it up but just put it in your shirt pocket for later.

The other thing about Cuban funerals is that there is no excuse for not turning up because the funeral home stays open around the clock as a sign of respect, and family members take turns to stay the night. My mother takes her turn and so do all my aunts and uncles and even more distant relatives who have come to Banes so they can farewell *Abuela*. I can't understand why they do this, why they can't go to sleep and then come back the next morning, but one of my cousins says that it's to make sure the dead are not left alone as they get ready to go to Heaven. It means if you can't sleep, you can pop down to the funeral home at any time, even at three in the morning, and sit with the sleepy relatives for a couple of hours, and gossip about whatever you want. With any luck, if you hang around long enough, someone will go and make another round of *cafecitos*.

This is not an easy task nowadays. My mother says that *antes del Triunfo*, that chronological line that divides everything in Cuba, this was not a big problem because, even if you were poor, there was always plenty of coffee and plenty of cigars to go around at funerals, but now coffee is rationed, so it's a struggle finding enough to make sure everyone who turns up gets at least one cup. If you are in luck, you may be able to go to the big building on what used to be the American side of Banes, where the revolutionary supply offices are, and make a case about how your relative has died and you need extra rations of coffee for the funeral home, and maybe, maybe, they will give you permission to get extra coffee from the grocer. Even then, my mother says, you have to keep an eye on who comes in because she reckons there are some people in town now who turn up at funerals all the time, even if they only vaguely know the family, so they can have a *cafecito*.

7 · *LA CURANDERA*

My stomach has been playing up again. I wake up with a stomach-ache—an *empacho*—feeling queasy, and with what may or may not be a slight fever. In most other places, I now know, you get a stomach-ache, some indigestion and a little nausea and you live with it. Not in Cuba. Here, the first thing your mother does is look you in the eyes, touch your stomach to see if it feels lumpy, check for a fever, and then she takes you to see a *curandera*, a kind of healer who will use her powers to make you feel okay again. There are various *curanderas* around Banes but my mother always goes to the one who lives about half an hour's walk from home because, my mother says, she is the best. I don't know how you compare *curanderas* but if my mother says she is the best, then she is the best.

This *curandera* is not only good at making your stomach-aches go away—I hope—but she can do much, much more because she is also a bit of a *santera*, which means she is well above your average healer. I am sure she can communicate with the great gods of Afro-Cuban *santería*, the religion brought over from Africa by the slaves, which means this *curandera* can also help solve marital problems, putting a spell on those who have done something wrong, like husbands who sleep with women who are not their wives. She can take away spells too, and importantly, she can tell mothers how to protect their new babies from *mal de ojo*, the evil eye. But what she does best, or what she does most often, is cure stomach-aches. She is an *empacho* expert.

Don't get me wrong. It's not that Cubans don't believe in medicine, or that there is a shortage of doctors. On the contrary, Fidel says Cubans have never been healthier. Thanks to the Revolution, there are now more doctors in Cuba than anywhere else in the entire world, he says, unlike in capitalist countries where there is always a shortage. Still, my mother takes my brother and me to the *curandera* whenever we don't feel well. I don't mind. I know from experience that to see one of those revolutionary doctors Fidel is talking about you have to go to the polyclinic and then queue for hours until one of the doctors is free to see you. On the other hand, I know that when you go to see the *curandera*, you don't have to wait. She is waiting for you.

Now, as my mother and I walk to see the *curandera*, I tell her that my *empacho* appears to be getting better. I feel fine now, I say, but she isn't listening—we are going to see the *curandera* regardless, whether Fidel approves or not. We haven't come all this way for nothing, my mother says. The house where the *curandera* lives is what Cubans would call *humilde pero honrada*. Humble but proud. And sure enough, as we approach the house, there she is, waiting for us. She is standing just inside the doorway, a huge woman with caramel-coloured skin who seems to be, to my eyes at least, really old. At least forty, I think, as she welcomes us with a wide smile and an apology that she cannot offer my mother *un cafecito* because, she says to my mother with knowing eyes, her ration has run out. It strikes me that everyone says the same thing. Inside, it smells of tobacco, coffee and the unmistakable scent of Cuban guavas. It is the smell of the tropics.

This is not the first time I have been in here and it won't be the last, and every time it feels kind of strange. It's too dark, but somehow very peaceful at the same time. Inside the *humilde pero honrada* house time seems to stand still. Even the scorching Caribbean sun seems to know better and doesn't dare enter, so that it's not only dark but cool. As my mother and the *curandera* chat about small town worries—they are talking about the queues, everyone always complains about the queues—I look around the small front room that serves as both sitting room, waiting room and consultation room. And there at the back, as I knew it would be, I can see up on the wall the small altar that this *curandera*, like all *curanderas*, has set up with a foot-high plaster statue of San Lazaro, the *santería* saint that is supposed to heal physical as well as spiritual pain. He looks so skinny you can see his rib cage, and he has bandages on his body and head, open wounds on his side; he supports himself on crutches of some sort, looking in absolute pain but resigned to a life of martyrdom. Next to him is his faithful dog, a skinny mongrel that stands right beside his leg looking up at the totally exhausted face of San Lazaro while licking one of the wounds. It's scary and I suspect I am going to have a nightmare tonight that involves San Lazaro and his mongrel.

On the altar just in front of the statue of San Lazaro there are a couple of lit candles giving out a warm glow, and next to them I can see a small glass which should have some rum in it, a couple of medium sized cigars whose aroma I can smell even from here, and a handful of bananas, stark yellow but quickly turning black.

And then, on the wall just behind the San Lazaro altar, there is a different kind of altar: it's a picture of Fidel wearing his trademark military cap and staring into space, as if challenging the Americans to come and get him, which is after all what he is always doing whenever he is on television or the radio. It's the type of picture you find in almost every house in Cuba, with an inscription underneath that says, *Fidel—esta es tu casa.* Fidel, this is your house. I don't need to tell you that there is no picture of Fidel in our house, and no promise that our house is his either.

By now my mother has finished gossiping with the *curandera,* who comes over to me and asks me to lie down on my back on a kind of canvas folding bed by one of the windows. She then asks me to take my shirt and singlet off and to lower my pants a little, so she can feel my stomach. I do as I am told, thinking that the one thing you must never do is disobey a *curandera*—unless you want to end up like San Lazaro, with wounds and a dog that keeps licking them. Her hands are leathery and I can feel the roughness of her skin as she moves them across and up and down my stomach, all the while mumbling something to my mother that I cannot understand. Truth is, I don't want to know what she is saying.

I look at the San Lazaro altar and at the Fidel photograph high up on the wall and think about something I heard one of my uncles say: that the Revolution doesn't have any time for *curanderas* and *santería.* My uncle should know, of course, because he is a big shot in the local Communist Party. He says *curanderas* and *santeras* are a leftover from the bad old days, from the days of capitalism and exploitation. Just like Catholicism, *santería* is meant to keep the poor in their place. It will take time, my uncle says, but the Revolution will prove those *santeras* wrong. My mother always listens politely to my uncle because he is so much more educated than she is and because he is important, but when it comes to *curanderas* she ignores him. She is still doing what a lot of other Cubans do—without making a fuss, she visits the *curandera* whenever it's required.

That is why we are inside the house of the *curandera*, who is now feeling my stomach. I can see she is almost done because she goes out and returns with a bunch of *yerba buena*, the Cuban herb used to ward off evil spirits. She is gently moving the bunch across my stomach and then in the air, and as she does, I can smell the pungent aroma of the herbs, and it's almost as if she has gone into a trance, her eyes closed, her smile gone, looking mighty serious as she mumbles something I can't make out. She then raises the herbs into the air one last time, waves them around vigorously, sets them aside and opens her eyes again. She smiles at me, asks me to get up and put my shirt and singlet back on, and then speaks softly to my mother, who takes a revolutionary *peso* note from her purse and hands it to the *curandera*, who doesn't charge anything, I suspect, because there is nothing to spend money on, but accepts any donation you can make. Preferably some ground coffee.

As we walk out of the house I can still smell the *yerba buena* on me but my stomach-ache is gone and I am not nauseous any more. I tell my mother, who smiles at me knowingly. Then she sends me to school.

8 · ALL IN THE FAMILY

It's Christmas Eve—*Nochebuena*—and there must be at least fifty people at the old family house in Presidente Zayas Avenue. The place is bursting at the seams, there are so many people in here. All of my uncles and my aunts and their children and even some of the neighbours. My uncle Tony has come all the way from Havana, as he does every year, and my aunt Adelina and my uncle Rogelio, who live in the mining town of Nicaro, are here too. There is music in the background, but it wouldn't be Cuba if there wasn't music somewhere in the background. It is probably a cha-cha-cha or one of those *son montunos* that have become so popular, but no one is dancing yet. That will come later, after dinner. Everyone seems to be too busy talking all at once, which is the Cuban way, and talking as loudly as they can, which is also the Cuban way, because that is the only way to be heard.

My mother and my aunts have managed to find enough tables and chairs for almost every adult to be able to sit down for dinner, while most of the younger children, like my brother, are too busy running around the house and darting in and out and occasionally falling down and crying and then getting up again, for anyone to pay too much attention. My cousin Tonito and I, who are older, get to sit down. I don't know what Tonito is thinking—probably that he'd rather be running around with the younger children because it is a lot more fun—but as I sit here, squashed between some of my other older cousins, I think how I have never seen so much food or so many people looking and sounding so happy.

I don't know how my mother and my aunts managed to do it because, as I have said, there is not much food anywhere in the shops any more, not even if it's your turn to buy groceries at the *bodega*, but they have come up with quite a feast. There is plenty of *congrí*, which one of my aunts made with rice and black beans and even bits of pork belly; and there is *yuca*, a tuber that you boil until it's tender and then immediately smother in a *mojito* made with lots of garlic, oil and lemon juice; and there is even a giant salad of lettuce, red tomatoes and big green tomatoes, which taste really tart but which my mother says have many more vitamins than ripe tomatoes. And because this is Cuba and because this is *Nochebuena*, there is also pork. A whole pig, in fact, that has been roasted slowly in a pit through the day and which has now been cut into large chunks and placed on big platters that get passed around so everyone can have not just some of the moist meat but also some of the crackling, because it's not a Cuban feast unless you have some *pellejito*.

Later, there will be dessert, probably *casquitos de guayaba*, which my mother makes using the pulp of the guava fruit and about twenty tonnes of sweet Cuban sugar, so much, in fact, that you can feel your teeth dancing. There will be some white-coloured cheese imported from Bulgaria that goes just right with the guava, and Polish apples and pears cut into small pieces so that everyone can have a taste since these are fruits we very rarely see in Cuba, and some grapes, which are also rare and therefore strictly rationed. All this will be followed by Spanish nougat—*turrón*—which is without doubt the highlight of my *Nochebuena*.

My father and my uncles, meanwhile, have collected enough beer and Cuban rum over the past few weeks to last a month, or at least to last through *Nochebuena*; you can easily tell that most of the men have been drinking for some hours already—while roasting the pig in the spit—and making a sizeable dent in the supplies. You can tell because they are all happier and louder than normal, and because even my uncle Papi, who is more reserved because he is so busy working for the Revolution, will come over to where Tonito and I are and give us a hug and say things like, My, how much you have grown in the last year! *Ya eres un hombrecito.* You are now a little man, which is just what boys our age want to hear.

It's been a long day for the males in the García household, especially for my father, who has become the family expert at what has to be the most symbolically *macho* chore of the day— and the most gruesome. He has become the pig slaughterer.

Children are never allowed to watch this ritual, of course, but now that I am older I am determined to see what happens, so I find a hiding place right under the stairs at the back of the house, which is raised high from the ground. I know that if I am discovered down here by my mother or one of my aunts, they will send me out to play on the street with the other children. Killing is not for children, my aunt Nidia will say, and shoo me away. So I lie on my stomach on the dry, powdery ground, watching through the timber slats as my father and my uncles put the finishing touches to a huge pit they have dug in the ground, where a fire has started to take and where, later on, the pig will be roasted, in the traditional Cuban way. But now, it's *la hora de matar el puerco.* Time to kill the pig.

My father and my uncles are sweating from all that digging under this boiling hot Cuban sun, even though, if you believe the calendar, it's supposed to be winter. They have a little break and drink a beer to cool down, but then it's time to get back to work. My father moves to the corner where the pig, which was bought a few days ago from a farm somewhere outside Banes, is tied to a post with a long piece of rope. It's a massive pig and a happy one, always eating scraps and making noises that make you think he doesn't have much to worry about, at least for now. But as soon as my father gets closer, the pig goes quiet, looks up from the mud that has been building up in that corner of the yard and starts to back up against the fence. I am sure he knows he is about to be killed because suddenly, with a loud grunting noise that scares me rigid, the big pig tries to get away, running between my father's legs, which is futile because the pig is tied to the rope and no matter how hard it tries, it can't go any further than the length of the rope. It cannot escape.

It is only now that I realise my father is carrying a huge, shiny knife that he has kept half hidden by his side. Then he stands behind the pig, which is squealing really loudly now, holds the animal by the neck and with one swift move, so quick I almost miss it, he lifts the pig up by its front legs and plunges the knife right into the pig's lower chest. Straight into the heart, I assume. It's then that the pig gives the loudest squeal of all, an angry squeal, the squeal of death. I am sure it can be heard across half of Banes. It's the scariest sound I have ever heard.

Everything is quiet for a second, but my father keeps holding the pig because he has done this before, at other *Nochebuenas*, and he knows that any moment now the pig will try to run away again in a last desperate attempt to stay alive. My father holds the animal really close to his chest and all I can see is a long stream of blood coming out of the pig's neck; one of my uncles collects the blood in a big pan to make *morcilla* sausages later on.

It's the same pig we will eat later tonight, after it has been gutted, then shaved with boiling water and a knife, and then rubbed all over with plenty of salt and juice from bitter oranges. Then they will stitch the pig up, stick a long pole into its back-side, through the now-empty rib area and out of its mouth, and mount it on bricks over the fiery pit. It will take hours before it's cooked and before the rest of the family arrives, wearing their best clothes, ready to eat, drink and celebrate another *Nochebuena*. Just before the pig is taken into the house to be chopped up into smaller pieces, my cousins and my brother fight each other to see who is going to eat the crunchy, garlicky, lemony pig's tail— *el rabito*—that everyone reckons is the best part of the *puerco*. This year I am not interested in *el rabito*, and when my uncle Rodolfo asks me why not, I tell him that I am not hungry right now. Next year, I say. Next year.

In our family, *Nochebuena* has always been a big deal but I guess that is the case for most other Cuban families. It's not that we are deeply religious or anything like that—far from it—but on 24 December just about every member of the family and a few distant relatives and the occasional neighbour will turn up as if by magic at the house in Presidente Zayas Avenue to celebrate Christmas Eve. It's always been like that, says my mother. As they sit at the long table that is really several long tables put together, there is always talk about past *Nochebuenas* and I realise that everyone seems to remember the *Nochebuena* of 24 December 1959 as among the best, coming just months after I was born and a year almost to the day the *barbudos* deposed Batista.

It must have been special because my mother has a photograph of that particular night that she has carried with her around the world. It's a black and white photograph taken in

64

the backyard of the house, with a backdrop of palm fronds. All her brothers and sisters are in the photograph, linking arms and smiling for the camera. There is my uncle Manuel Enrique, who would die of leukaemia, a painful and slow death some years later, before I really got to know him. My uncle Victor, who fought in the Sierra Maestra with Fidel and the other *barbudos*, is in the photograph too, wearing his gala army uniform and linking arms with my aunt Adelina, who looks so proud of him; and my uncle Tony, looking prosperous in a white linen suit, and my aunt Mirta, glamorous in her floral dress, smiling her big smile. Then there is my mother, in a black party dress, looking young and happy and full of optimism because, after all, 1960 is just around the corner, and everyone is confident that everything is going to be all right. Of course, sometimes you can read too much into a photograph.

★

My aunt Mirta and her husband, my uncle Rodolfo—or Offo, as my brother calls him—are coming to live in Banes. My brother and I think it's terrific because of all my aunts and uncles, Mirta and Rodolfo are by far the most fun. I think my aunt is a little crazy in a lovable kind of way, always laughing, always in a hurry and always making deals, even when there is nothing to make deals with, while Rodolfo is laid back and loves cracking jokes; whenever he visits, always smelling of his American Old Spice cologne, he gives my brother and me some money, which we save even though in reality there is not much to spend it on.

I don't realise this at the time but their decision to move to Banes is both an uncharacteristic admission of defeat and the start of a process that will eventually tear my mother's close-knit family apart. But for now, all I can think of is how great it is that my aunt and uncle are moving here. Until recently they owned a big store in San Germán, a town not far from Banes, where they used to sell just about everything imaginable, from sofa suites and modern American washing machines that even help you dry your shirts and trousers, to fancy leather shoes that you put on to go out dancing. It was the biggest shop in the town and for my parents, whose shop was much smaller, it was something to aim for. But now, Mirta and Rodolfo don't own the shop any more because all the big shops in Cuba belong to the People. They work there but they don't own the place—they don't even manage the shop, as the Revolution has appointed to the position of administrator a woman who used to be one of the employees (and not a very good one, my mother adds with disdain); 'administrator' is the title they give the new bosses. You can tell just by looking at them that it has been a big blow to Mirta and Rodolfo. My happy aunt is not as happy as she used to be, and my laidback uncle seems much more distant than I can ever recall. There is an air about them of absolute defeat which even a boy can recognise. All that hard work for nothing, is what they say.

I can't even begin to imagine how they managed to shift to Banes because moving from one town to another is close to impossible in Cuba nowadays, unless you have permission from the government. Moving houses isn't easy either, because no one owns their own house any more, even if they paid for it. All the houses in Cuba now belong to the Revolution. It means you can stay in the house that used to be yours for as long as you want but you can't sell it—and you can't buy another one. Sometimes, however, you can swap houses—*permutar*—but this takes a long time and lots of paperwork and, of course, you have to find someone who is happy to make the swap with you, which is the hardest thing of all. And if you are moving to another town, like my uncle and aunt, then you also need permission to apply for another job, which can take forever, even though now everyone is really employed by the government. To make ends meet, my aunt has set up a small business at home cooking *harina de maíz*—semolina—which she then sells door to door around Banes, or she exchanges the *harina* for other food or used clothing or anything she thinks may come in handy.

The house my aunt and uncle have managed to find in Banes is a big, almost-new timber house on the outskirts, near the main road that takes you out of the town on the way to Holguin. Inside, the house is full of light with plenty of space and lots of rooms, including a big living room where no one ever sits and a dining room with huge windows and a big, solid table and ornate chairs that, according to one of my aunts, were made a long time ago and shipped to Cuba directly from Spain. Compared to our house, it's a palace.

Outside, there is a huge yard, the biggest I have ever seen, with enough room for a chook pen and even a corner to raise a little pig or two, says my uncle, smacking his lips in anticipation of the feast that he is sure will come. In the yard there is a big *mamoncillo* tree that will inevitably become the highlight of our visits to my aunt's new house. My brother and I love climbing the spreading branches and then using a long stick to whack the branches until the *mamoncillos* fall down, sometimes exploding when they hit the dry ground below. My mother, on the other hand, hates the *mamoncillo* tree because the juice from the fruit stains our white shirts and shorts, and in revolutionary Cuba you have got to look after your clothes, *chico*, because you know very well that you can't just pop into the local shop and buy a new pair of trousers willy-nilly. God knows, she says in exasperation, when they will ship children's trousers again! My brother and I just keep whacking the branches with the long sticks.

My aunt and uncle are sharing the house with uncle Rodolfo's father, whom we all call Prado, which is really his surname. Prado used to live part of the year with them in San Germán and is now coming back to Banes too. In his seventies, he is an old Asturian who doesn't say much, hates noisy children and likes to eat every night at six o'clock on the dot so that he can get to bed early and wake up again the next day at the same time as the roosters. I don't know why he does this because my uncle says all Prado does during the day is sit under the mango trees in the backyard.

Every Sunday night without fail, we meet at my aunt's new place for dinner. We sit at the solid old table and eat the same dish: a *garbanzada*, a chickpea stew that is Prado's favourite and that is supposed to have bits of ham and potatoes and meat in it but which, like everything else, has been adapted to the new socialist reality. In other words, there are chickpeas in there and some stringy meat but no ham and no potatoes. Some Sunday nights after dinner, we go to the sitting room and wait expectantly for my uncle to take out his American slide projector, a big, bulky apparatus that looks so modern and sophisticated and ... capitalist. Then he takes out his big box of Kodak slides, all shiny and transparent and full of colour and light and carefully catalogued, before turning off the lights and switching on the machine.

There, reflected on the white wall, are images of a recent past that now seems almost prehistoric—pictures of my uncle and aunt and even Prado, everyone looking younger, standing outside the San Germán shop and smiling for the camera with a sense of optimism and satisfaction that seems to burn through the slide itself. There are pictures of me as a baby in my uncle's arms, taken, I assume, on our regular visits to San Germán. In one, I am wearing an olive-green *barbudos* uniform which was made by my aunt. There are pictures of my parents, my father still sporting his

Errol Flynn moustache that, he says jokingly, used to drive the girls crazy. There are pictures of other family members on my mother's side, and one where everyone is looking happy and well dressed, sitting at a long table somewhere drinking Hatuey beers, ready to get stuck into the roasted suckling pig that sits on a huge platter in the middle of the table, right there, so colourful it feels as if you could just stretch your arm and touch it.

But despite the slide nights, I can tell that our Sunday dinners are becoming more and more serious as the months progress. After dinner, as my aunt and my mother start taking the plates to the kitchen to do the washing up—which is women's work, of course—my uncle Rodolfo and my father sit around the big old table talking about how things are getting worse—*las cosas, coño, cada vez se ponen peor*—and how there is no hope in sight that *El Caballo*, as my uncle refers to Fidel sometimes, will see the error of his communist ways and turn back the clock, which I figure means returning the shop to my uncle so he is happy again. Sometimes, when they get talking about these things, they tell me to go and play outside with my brother because these are discussions for grown-ups only. *Vete, vete a jugar*, they say. Go out and play, and I do as I am told but of course I think I know what's going on. I can tell by the way they speak almost in a whisper, scared that someone will overhear their conversation. I can tell what they are planning. I can tell that my uncle wants to leave Cuba, that he and my aunt are ready to apply for permission to go to New York, and he wants my parents and my brother and me to follow them.

My father, who knows about these things, says Guardalavaca, which is only about half an hour by road from Banes, is the best beach in the whole of Cuba. No argument. But most people in Cuba don't know that because they all think the best beach in Cuba is Varadero, which is far away in Matanzas province, closer to Havana. My father says that *antes del Triunfo*, rich Americans discovered Varadero and started building huge holiday mansions along the shore, and then they built cabarets and bars and restaurants and large hotels, which then attracted lots of other rich Americans, and plenty of rich honeymooning Cubans too. They were too lazy to bother travelling further east to Guardalavaca, which is why there are no big mansions here. There is, however, a hotel with cabins where you can stay overnight and a big restaurant with a covered dining area that has sweeping views of the beach, and where they play music on Saturday nights. Some nights they also sell beer in large cardboard containers but you have to queue for a long time. I am sure that happens in Varadero too.

In Guardalavaca the water is bright, blue and very warm, the sand is sparkling white, and right along the foreshore there are huge spreading trees known as *uvas caletas* that provide plenty of shade; we children can hide and run around them without losing sight of our parents. Even the name of the place is exotic. It means 'Hide the cow' and a friend at school, Jorgito, explained that it's got something to do with Christopher Colombus arriving at the beach one day and, like all colonialists, trying to steal the cows that belonged to the local Indians. I don't believe my friend because I know for a fact that the Cuban Indians didn't have any cows, but it's a good story and I am prepared to give Jorgito the benefit of the doubt. He is my friend.

The worst thing about Guardalavaca, however, is getting there. There is a paved road that links Banes and Guardalavaca which, according to my father, was built by Batista *antes del Triunfo* but he says this to me very quietly and—again—assumes I will not be repeating such heresies to anyone. I don't quite believe my father, though, because at school we have learned that Batista was just a crook who pinched all the money in Cuba while ordinary Cubans went hungry. The problem is not the road but the fact that we need to catch a bus to get there, and buses are rare these days. So if you can hitch a ride on a truck or even a tractor you do it, but trucks are rare too, and when one comes along it is usually full of young soldiers doing compulsory military service—*servicio militar*—to protect us from the Americans who are, as we speak, getting ready to invade Cuba and destroy the Revolution.

To get to Guardalavaca, you queue for a bus ticket and then you wait in the queue for the bus to arrive and then you wait for the driver to go to the bathroom, to wash his hands, get himself a *cafecito*, to flirt with the girl at the ticket counter, to chat to his mates the mechanics, and then, finally, to get back on the bus. Sometimes, just as you are getting ready to board the bus after waiting for a long time, they will announce that, *compañeros*, the bus is broken down and we will have to wait until someone goes and finds the mechanic, who will then have to spend some time trying to find out if there is a spare part somewhere in Banes that can be used to get the bus back on the road. And of course, this is going to take a long time because if the bus is one of those old American ones no spare parts will be available because, as you know, the Americans are no longer selling Cuba any spare parts. No, *señor*, the Yankees want to make Cubans wait and wait and wait for the bus to be fixed before we can get to the beach.

The funny thing is that the buses that break down all the time are not the old American ones, but the new ones Fidel has bought from Czechoslovakia, which come with snow chains because, according to one of my father's friends, someone in

Czechoslovakia told the Cubans that all the buses come with snow chains, regardless of where they are being sent to in the vast and rapidly expanding communist world. Even to someone my age, it is obvious that the reason these proletarian buses break down so often is because there is no snow in Cuba. If there was, we could use the snow chains and then everything would be all right. I am sure Fidel is working on that too.

All this means that visiting Guardalavaca can be quite an expedition, even if my father can sometimes find a way of getting tickets and getting the entire family on board without having to queue for too long—the benefits of having old friends on the buses, he says, winking knowingly. *El que tiene padrino*, he says . . . In Cuba, it's known as having *palanca*, which means you know someone who knows someone who is happy to do you a favour this time because you will do them a favour later. I am not sure it's a very revolutionary thing, this *palanca*, and sometimes I feel it is unfair because all those other people have been waiting for the bus for a long time; but on the other hand, I am going to Guardalavaca . . .

We normally come to the beach with the entire family— my brother, my parents, my uncles and aunts and cousins— because in Cuba you always do things with the family. And you always pack lots and lots of stuff to take to the beach, even if you don't need it. Just in case. This time we are staying overnight, all of us squashed into two of the cabins at the hotel, which are clean and have comfortable beds, except someone has stolen the light fittings, so that only the bare bulbs are left. The doors don't close well, either, because someone has stolen the locks. Still, I don't think we should complain. These are holidays for the masses, for the People, as they say on the radio. Not like before the Revolution, when only the rich could have holidays like this, they say. Luckily for Cubans, Fidel arrived and now everyone can take holidays to Guardalavaca. If you are lucky to get a ticket that gets you a seat on the bus, and if the bus can make it to Guardalavaca, of course.

As we settle under one of the huge trees that sprout out almost miraculously from the bright white sand, my mother and my aunts produce another miracle: crackers that we call *galleticas*, some bread, bananas and mangoes, an avocado for the salad, and a can or two of pressed meat which has been sent to Cuba by our fraternal friends in Hungary and which is available on the quiet, under the counter, if you know the right people. One of my aunts says the pressed meat smells funny wherever it comes from—*¡de donde sea!*—and it comes surrounded with some gooey jelly which tastes awful and, really, we'd rather have a big Cuban steak, some *platanos fritos*, a bit of *congrí* or—my mouth is watering as I think it—perhaps some pork: *masitas de puerco*. We don't complain, mind you. How could we? We are in Guardalavaca, under a bright blue sky, shaded from the sun by the branches of the *uva caleta*, eating pressed, canned meat that has been sent by our kind communist friends in Eastern Europe, who are working hard to ensure that all peace-loving peoples of the world are free from American imperialism so they, too, can enjoy travelling in those fraternal buses with snow chains.

The only problem with the food is that now we have stuffed our faces, we can't get into the water. I don't know where this rule came from or when, but ever since I can remember, all across Cuba, if you have lunch, your mother will not allow you to get back into the water for at least an hour, or until you have digested all your food and don't feel full any more. Otherwise, my mother says, you can get a *patatú*, a seizure that turns your face purple and kills you. And not even the best *curandera* in all of Cuba can save you! I know people at school who have gone back into the water right after eating and they have survived, but I am sure it was just plain old luck. Still, as my cousins and my brother and I sit around, bored, waiting for the clock to tick, tick, tick until an hour has passed, we curse our parents, we curse science, we curse those Americans, and we curse ourselves for having eaten so much of that gooey Hungarian pressed meat.

9 · RATIONING TALES

The most important book in all of Cuba, the book you must guard with your very life, is *la libreta*—the ration book that every Cuban family needs to be able to buy food. It's something you learn from a very early age—you take care of *la libreta*, which is inevitably accompanied by *la jaba*, an all-purpose shopping bag my mother has made from old canvas that reeks of optimism and unfulfilled promise. You never know when you will need your *jaba*, to buy whatever is available, so it comes with you all the time. You, the *jaba* and the *libreta*.

My parents say rationing is not something they ever thought they would see in Cuba but they were wrong because now almost everything is rationed. That is the way it has been since 1962 when Fidel announced that rationing would be introduced, but only for a year, because the Americans don't want to sell Cuba anything any more, which means the shelves are empty in the shops. He says rationing is the only way the Revolution can ensure everyone has exactly the same amount of food to eat, which is the socialist way. I cannot understand why Fidel doesn't just buy more food from our Russian friends but I guess they have rationing of their own.

If the topic comes up at school, the teachers tell us that the *libreta* is the price we pay for being independent and anti-imperialist and, besides, it means everyone has enough food not to go hungry. I am not so sure about this and I wonder whether Fidel has his own *libreta* and whether he has to queue like my mother does so she can buy half a pound of black beans. But I keep these thoughts to myself. It's not something you say out loud and, anyway, we all know that Fidel is busy, day in and day out, defending the Revolution so it would be quite unpatriotic of me even to think about such things.

In fact there are two ration books in Cuba: one is for food, which is the one with the most pages, and the other one is for non-food items like clothes and shoes and bedsheets or towels. The second *libreta* is a joke, according to my mother, because there is never anything to buy in the shops. She should know— she owns a shop. The *libreta* for food is the one you must take real care of because if you lose it or someone steals it, you are in big trouble. Just getting a new *libreta* from the central planning office can take weeks, and during that time you have to rely on your family or neighbours to get something to eat, and of course they never have enough. No one in Banes ever has enough, or at least no one I know, rationing or not.

In a move that would later strike me as Orwellian if only Fidel had not banned George Orwell's books for being counter-revolutionary, officially the ration book is not called a *Libreta de Racionamiento*, it's called a *Libreta de Abastecimientos* which, roughly translated, means a 'supply book', hinting at an abundance which, even a child can tell you, most certainly is not there. With the *libreta* a family like ours can buy a set amount of food which the government says is enough to keep us Cubans healthy and well-fed and alert should those Americans attempt to invade us. It means that every month, each person in our house is entitled to three pounds of rice, one and a half pounds of black beans, four ounces of ground coffee, three pounds of meat from the butcher, one toilet roll, one-quarter of a tube of toothpaste and, if you are old enough, two packets of cigarettes. Of course, you soon discover there is no guarantee that any of these goods will be in the shops, but if they are then that's what our family is entitled to, and that is what we get. If you eat all the food at once, then you are in trouble because you won't get any more until next month.

To make sure there are no anti-revolutionary acts like hoarding or pushing prices up, every family is allocated a *bodega*— a grocery store—where you must go once every fortnight to get your food. Same with the butcher shop and the bakery. You can't just buy stuff anywhere, even if you have the *libreta* with you, and that indispensable *jaba*. And despite having an allocated shop and an allocated day to go and buy your allocated goods, often you still have to queue. The queue I am in now is long. There must be at least twenty people ahead of me, almost all of them women because this is Cuba and even in revolutionary Cuba queuing for food is regarded as women's work. So, here they are, revolutionary Cuban women in flimsy housecoats, in floral dresses that have seen much, much better days, some with their hair in rollers, the rollers covered with a *pañueleta*, a brightly coloured headscarf that has become a very Cuban fashion accessory now that no one can buy hairspray.

Everyone has the *libreta*, everyone has a *jaba* and everyone knows each other. This is Banes, and everyone starts off in good humour, which is the Cuban way to cope with queues. But as the waiting drags on and on and on and the sun starts to really bite into your skin and make you sweat until you glisten, the jokes and the laughing and the *piropos* that the one or two men in the queue direct at passing *mulatas* give way to a resigned silence, which is also a very Cuban way to deal with queues like this one. Do you think that inside their heads they may be thinking counter-revolutionary thoughts? Like, when is this business of the *libretas* and the queues going to finish? Are you wondering whether all those *dirigentes*, those leaders of the Revolution who are always on television telling Cubans to work harder at building a socialist state, are also queueing right now? You'd better keep these thoughts in your head because they are dangerous. I look at my mother and ask, almost pleadingly, How much longer do we have to wait? It won't be long, she says, it won't be long, son. It's a white lie.

Sometimes you don't need the *libreta* to buy things. Sometimes shops receive additional goods and they are allowed to sell them freely, or *por la libre*, although the prices are still controlled by the government. It doesn't happen all that often, but whenever there is food being sold without rationing, the queues that form outside are even longer than the ones that form when something arrives at the *bodega* for sale with *la libreta*. Sometimes it doesn't matter what's for sale *por la libre*—you see a queue and you just jump on the end, *jaba* at the ready, to buy whatever is on offer. You do this because you can never be sure when food will be on sale again, and because if you have a surplus, you can always exchange whatever it is with other members of the extended family or with your neighbours. If you don't smoke, you get your packets of cigarettes and then exchange them with someone you know who does smoke but who doesn't need as much oil as you or who doesn't like chickpeas. True socialism, no? But you still have to queue.

Most of the time, what is sold *por la libre* is food that somehow isn't rationed probably because it is food most Cubans don't like much or know nothing about, like funny-smelling sardines from Yugoslavia. Or ham from Russia that comes in small tins. If you were thinking counter-revolutionary thoughts, which I most certainly am not, you would be asking why, fifty years after what at school we always call the Glorious October Revolution, Russians are eating such bad food instead of eating real ham and cheese like the Americans. *Antes del Triunfo*, my mother says, sounding surprisingly and dangerously subversive, Russian pressed ham was the sort of food we Cubans wouldn't even give to pigs . . . *Ni a los puercos.*

Every year there is talk that the *libreta* may come to an end because things are improving, because we are harvesting more sugarcane and selling more sugar to the capitalist countries in exchange for food, because Fidel promised . . . and every year the *libreta* remains.

Near our house there is a fish shop run by Jamaicans who speak Spanish with a funny accent. Every second day or so they get fish in, which I cannot quite understand because Banes is so close to the sea and you would think you could sell fish every day, but no one says anything because at least fish is not rationed. You don't need *la libreta*. On fish days the queue starts to form outside the shop long before the doors open. You don't know what kind of fish will be on sale but there will be fish. For what seems like hours, we stand outside in the sun listening to a couple of old Haitian women, with skin the colour of the darkest night, talk in a language my father tells me later is *patois*—a mixture of African and French, with the occasional Spanish word thrown in for good measure. There are quite a few Haitians and Jamaicans in Banes, most of whom arrived in Cuba sometime in the 1930s and 1940s to cut sugarcane for the old United Fruit Company.

Today, as we queue for fish, the sun is hotting up and everyone is sweating and getting more and more impatient, except for the Haitian ladies, who seem not to sweat and who cool themselves with old cardboard fans that my mother says used to be given away to promote cigarette brands or miracle constipation pills. *Antes del Triunfo*, she adds unnecessarily. We are all waiting to walk across the threshold of the small shop and into the cool dark interior, the not very well ventilated interior where the smell of fish is so overwhelming I feel like throwing up, which I don't do because I am on my way to becoming a man and only babies throw up.

My brother and I don't mind fish but often, by the time it's your turn in the queue, all that is left are fish heads. They are large and ugly and menacing but my father claims the fish heads are good because they are the tastiest and most nutritious part of the fish. See? This is where all the goodness is, he says, pointing at the fish heads with great enthusiasm. Tonight my father makes fish soup for dinner. Nutritious or not, it tastes horrible, but at least I get to suck on the fish eyes, which float on the top of the clear liquid like shrunken ping-pong balls.

My father likes to cook occasionally, which is something of a rarity for Cuban men of his generation. He will make a soup or a potage with black beans or lentils or, if he is truly inspired and if we have been lucky enough to score some at the butcher's, he will make pig's trotters, which used to be one of my favourite dishes until a neighbourhood friend told me that pig's trotters are the dirtiest parts of the pig, and how can you eat such things, *chico*? In revolutionary Cuba, as we work our way to socialism, you have got to experiment with whatever is available that day in the *bodega*, which explains why, on some other nights, we sit at the dining table eating tripe my ever-inventive father has prepared with a tomato and onion sauce. Like my mother, he says cooking was a lot easier and a lot more flavoursome back in the old days because you could buy proper meat and proper fish if you had the money, and you could pop down to the *bodega* any time and come back with herbs and spices and some pork fat to give the food some additional flavour. They paint a picture of abundance that seems to me totally unrealistic. I think they are exaggerating because they want me to believe that despite what I get told at school, not everything was bad in the days before Fidel.

That night when I go to bed, I keep thinking about ham, pink, fatty, smoky ham, which in truth I have tasted only at Christmas time when Fidel throws all caution to the wind and gives his revolutionary people a few grams of imported ham, probably from Canada. It's totally decadent and I wonder—in the quietness of my head—whether this is what other people in the world have for dinner every night.

10 · KINGS OF HAVANA

We are going to Havana. This will be only my second trip to Havana—the first time, when I was much younger, all four of us went because my father had to see a specialist and in Cuba all the good specialists are in Havana, no matter what anyone says. If you are sick, you pray to the Virgen de la Caridad del Cobre, and then go to Havana. This time, my father is staying home to look after the shop.

We are going to Havana to say goodbye to my uncle Rodolfo, my aunt Mirta and my cousin Carrie, who is not even three. More than a year after applying, they have been given permission to leave Cuba, flying straight from Havana to the United States in flights that my uncle says are known in Miami as freedom flights—*el puente de la libertad*—but not in Cuba, where they are just a planeload of *gusanos*. It's the only way to leave Cuba and you have to wait and wait and cross your fingers that there is no problem in the meantime.

I am sure I am going to miss my aunt and my uncle, especially my aunt Mirta, who can be so much fun with the way she talks really fast and how she manages to find presents for my brother and me even when there is nothing much to buy in the shops. But right now none of that is important to me because all I can think about is going to Havana; for a boy from Banes, that is quite a treat. Before we leave, my father sits my brother and me down and tells us, in the stern, low voice he reserves for serious occasions, that for the sake of our uncle and aunt, we have to behave when we get to Havana. Do you understand? he asks. You have to behave and that means you don't tell anyone that your aunt and uncle and cousin are leaving for *El Norte*.

I can't understand why this is such a big deal, but I don't care. It's a small price to pay, it seems to me, to be able to go to Havana.

Havana is huge compared to Banes and you can tell this as soon as the bus leaves the countryside behind and enters the city. And the closer we get to the centre, the taller the buildings become and the more people I see walking and queuing, and all I can think of is that I must be very, very careful not to get lost here because if I do, there is no way I could ever find my way back to Banes, even if I queued for days waiting for a bus ticket.

There are not too many queues where we are staying, though. Our home away from home is an apartment in Miramar, which I find out later is the most exclusive neighbourhood in all of Cuba. It was exclusive *antes del Triunfo* because this is where all the rich people built their mansions, not far from the beach, along wide, tree-lined streets that are called avenues and that look nothing like the streets and avenues of Banes. Few of those rich people are still around. Most of them left for *El Norte* a long time ago and their big houses and apartments now belong to the People—or to ambassadors and technicians from fraternal countries such as Russia and Poland, who seem to be everywhere when we go out later to walk the streets and enjoy the cool breeze that comes from the Straits of Florida.

The houses that now belong to the People really belong to people like my uncle Victor, my mother's oldest brother, who was a *barbudo* fighting in the Sierra Maestra with Fidel and who is now a senior officer in the army. I have only met him once, a long time ago, when he came to Banes to visit, but I know my mother talks fondly of him and his wife, whom I have never met. Now we are in his apartment and, let me tell you, it is huge. It's like something straight out of a movie, with big windows, a balcony, lots of furniture, a big fridge and even a television. It's so close to the beach you can hear the sound of the waves. The whole building is like this: downstairs, I discover, there are other families whose fathers are also defending the Revolution and their apartments are also huge, and most of the fathers who defend the Revolution have a car parked outside, or an army jeep with a driver comes in the morning and picks them up to take them to work.

My aunt and my two cousins, who are much younger than me, are great fun to be with and they make us feel welcome from the moment we arrive, showing us the rooms where we will sleep, my mother, brother and I on one huge, very comfortable bed; and my aunt Mirta, my uncle Rodolfo and my cousin Carrie in another room. It's like we are on holidays in the best place we have ever been to. And it is even better than the hotel cabins in Guardalavaca because here, no one has stolen the light fittings or the locks on the doors. The only person missing is my uncle Victor. He is busy defending the Revolution, which is something he does all the time, I think.

Before we go anywhere, my mother reminds us not to tell anyone that we are here to say goodbye to my aunt and uncle and cousin who are leaving for the United States. Don't tell anyone because if you do, then your uncle Victor can get into trouble. Pretend you are on holidays, she insists. I am happy to pretend. I keep thinking that it's a good thing all those rich *gusanos* left and these houses have been given over to 'certain people', as my uncle Rodolfo says, gesturing to us by placing two fingers on his shoulder as if he is in the army. He winks and we know exactly what he means . . .

We soon discover that in Havana you don't have to queue. Okay, that's not true. In Havana, like in Banes, everyone has to queue outside the shops or at the bus stop, but not if you live in a big apartment in Miramar. At my uncle's house there is a woman who comes every couple of days to clean the house and she has no problem buying things. A big, black woman with a big smile that shows a row of impeccably white teeth, she makes a note of everything we need in the apartment and then goes out to a special shop for people who are protecting the Revolution and who live in Miramar, and she comes back with huge bags full of things we don't get to see too often, if ever, in Banes. Like chicken legs and steaks and plantain and rice, and it's like paradise, says my mother, who can't believe her eyes. I imagine there is a huge miracle shop somewhere in Havana where the best revolutionaries can walk in without queuing and then buy anything they want. I picture mountains of ham in these shops, and huge boxes of apples and enormous cheeses from Spain, just waiting to be bought by our revolutionary heroes. Like my mother says: a miracle.

Today we have all decided to go to the zoo because everyone in Banes said you have to go to the zoo in Havana because it is a great place for children. It's my first visit to a zoo anywhere. It's the first time I see lions and elephants in real life and it's fun getting a running commentary from my uncle Rodolfo as we move from one cage to another, because he seems to have a joke about every animal, especially the monkeys. We still have to queue to buy some small sandwiches and a drink for lunch but we are having such a great time, no one complains.

At the end of the day, as dusk starts to fall, we wait outside the zoo gates with lots of other people for the bus that will take us back to Miramar. There is a long queue but by now we are used to queues. It'd be news if there wasn't a queue. Eventually we catch the bus and walk all the way to the back to take the only seats that are empty. The bus is packed, like all buses are in Cuba, but everyone is in good spirits because everyone has had a great time at the zoo, just like we did. There is an elderly lady sitting in the seat next to where I am standing and she starts talking to my brother and me, asking us where we are from. We tell her we are from Banes, which is in Oriente province, and she tells us how polite we seem to be and did we enjoy seeing the lions and the giraffe, which we did, and then she asks, What are you doing in Havana? And because I have had a great day at the zoo and I feel comfortable and happy, I point to where my mother is sitting and I say to the old lady, We are here to say goodbye to our uncle and our aunt; they are going to the United States. Then I realise that this is not what I am supposed to say, that I have been warned not to even mention *El Norte*.

The back of the bus falls silent. No one says anything. I look at my mother, who is pretending not to notice. I can see that my uncle Rodolfo is quiet too, and no one says anything at all for the next twenty minutes, until we get to our stop in Miramar and file out.

The next day my uncle Tony arrives to pick us up. He has an important position in the revolutionary government too, although I don't think he is as important as my uncle Victor because he lives in a smaller apartment and he doesn't have a woman who comes to clean and who brings special food from the special shop. But my uncle Tony must still be pretty important because, unlike any other Cuban I know, he is allowed to travel overseas, heading delegations to fraternal countries and sometimes even to capitalist countries in Europe. He goes overseas at least once a year, representing Cuba. What's more, my uncle Tony has a car. True, it is not an Italian Alfa Romeo, which is the car used by all the really important Communist Party *dirigentes* in Havana. It's a small Russian car given to him by the government because he is a good revolutionary and an important man and I decide right there and then that that is what I want to be when I grow up—a good revolutionary who is allowed to travel overseas representing Cuba and who is given a Lada. Or even better, one of those navy-coloured Alfa Romeos.

My uncle Tony says he is taking us on a tour of Havana so my mother and brother and me and my aunt Mirta and my cousin all pile into the small car, which smells brand new. The seats are covered in thin vinyl that gets really hot and sticky very soon, smelling a little like burnt rubber and giving me a headache. My uncle Tony thinks it will be fun for us to drive through the Havana tunnel which goes under Havana Bay and links La Habana Vieja, the old city, to the new and modern eastern part of the city, popping up magically at the other end. No one mentions this at the time but later, when we get back home to my uncle Victor's apartment in Miramar and I tell my uncle Rodolfo, he says the tunnel was built by Batista when he was still president. Built by capitalists? Really? I don't know whether my uncle Rodolfo is serious or just joking, like he always does.

We enjoy being driven around Havana, especially since there are few other cars on the wide streets and avenues that lead us around the Malecón and then through the Vedado area and, later, across the Almendares River and back to Miramar. My uncle Tony tells me with a conspiratorial wink that Fidel has a house right here in Miramar too, but that in reality no one knows for sure where he stays on any given night because he likes to move around all the time, from house to house and apartment to apartment, to make sure he fools those Americans who want to kill him. It's a great story, which I will repeat to my friends when I get back home to Banes. As we pass yet another big billboard telling Cubans to become even better revolutionaries, I look out the window and wonder what the people we see on the streets are thinking, standing in long lines waiting for buses that never come. And I wonder what they would say if they knew that this brand new government Lada is packed with *gusanos*.

The highlight of the day comes when uncle Tony takes us all to Coppelia, the huge new ice cream place right in the middle of Havana's most fashionable neighbourhood, the Vedado. Everyone in Cuba knows about the Coppelia because since it opened it has become the most popular place in all of revolutionary Havana. And every child knows, of course, that the Coppelia serves more than one hundred different flavours of ice cream, and that you don't need *la libreta*! Of course, you have to queue—and it's a really long queue—so we stand in line for what seems like hours, inching our way closer to the door so we can order our ice creams and go back out to find a table under the huge shady trees that surround the circular structure that to me looks more like a stranded spaceship than the most famous ice cream shop in all of Cuba.

If I wasn't living in Cuba, I would probably have spent my waiting time trying to make up my mind which of the more than one hundred flavours of ice cream I was going to order when I finally got to the long counter at the front. But I know that when it's our turn to order, there won't be one hundred flavours to pick from. Or even fifty. Or even twenty. That's the way it is in Cuba. You get promised one hundred or more flavours of ice cream but you know, from the start, that there will only be two or three to choose from. If you are lucky. In this case we are not lucky and we never expected to be. All of us walk out of the Coppelia licking strawberry flavoured ice creams which, of course, was the only flavour left.

11 · OPIUM OF THE MASSES

My parents are not what you'd call devout Catholics. As my father likes to point out, he and my mother didn't even get married in church! Mind you, as soon as my brother and I were born, they rushed to the Catholic church in Banes to have us both baptised. Like most Cubans do. I figure it's like a form of insurance. You know, just in case . . . The reason this is on my mind now is because my parents, who don't go to church, who don't pray at night and who don't even say grace when we sit down to dinner, and never will, have decided that it's the right time for my brother and me to start attending Sunday mass. This is not what I call good news.

But you don't go to mass, I say to my mother, trying to explain to her as best I can just how hypocritical her stance seems to be. I think my case is pretty strong but she is determined. She just doesn't understand anything about religion. Like every other school child in Cuba, I *know* that religion is bad. I know that Karl Marx called it the Opium of the Masses, a capitalist tool designed to keep the poor in their place. That's what Marx said anyway.

I also know that priests are parasites, thieves and fascists, which is why Fidel had them all shipped back to Spain as soon as he could. It's why the Revolution closed all Catholic schools, the Catholic radio stations and the Catholic newspapers. And it's why Fidel abolished Holy Week and replaced it with the much more revolutionary Playa de Girón Week. Instead of spending time on our knees praying for the resurrection of Jesus Christ, good revolutionaries now spend what used to be Holy Week celebrating the Great Anti-Imperialist Victory of Playa de Girón, which is what Cubans call the Bay of Pigs, the site where hundreds of Cuban exiles landed in 1961 to try to topple Fidel. Of course, my textbooks don't call them exiles. They are called mercenaries, paid and trained by the Americans, and so lacking in true revolutionary courage that Fidel had no trouble capturing them within a couple of days of the landing. Then they were paraded in front of the television cameras for all Cubans to see what a mercenary looked like, before being sent to prison until the United States agreed to take them back in exchange for medicines. There was a priest among the invaders, too.

Before my mother got this crazy idea about church, my brother and I used to get up early on Sundays, have breakfast, dress and then join every other child in the neighbourhood for the matinee at the cinema that happens to be—can you believe this—just across the plaza from the church. On Sundays the cinema shows cartoons—*los muñequitos*—and old American black and white serials like *Tarzan*, *Dick Tracy* and *The Shadow*, all dubbed into Spanish. And yes, you guessed right, the *muñequitos* and the old serials are shown at exactly the same time as Sunday mass. One of my aunts says this is deliberate, to discourage children from going to church. She says that in some other towns they have started staging puppet shows and giving away sweets and soft drinks to children just outside the church, right when mass is supposed to start. No such luck in Banes.

Still, much as I try to negotiate with my mother so we can skip mass and join our friends at the cinema instead, the response is always the same: *No, señor.* Never mind that going to church in Banes on a Sunday—or any other day for that matter—is either for losers or for *gusanos*, which is kind of the same thing when you think about it. Real revolutionaries don't pray; they volunteer to cut sugarcane on Sundays. Never mind that some of my friends at school will tease me about going to church and our all too obvious lack of revolutionary conviction. Never mind that sometimes, when it is quiet inside the church—say, when everyone is supposed to be praying—you can hear the soundtrack of whatever old serial is being shown at the cinema on the other side of the square.

Even during mass there are not too many people in here. Only half the pews are occupied and most are occupied by old and frail white women who still wear a black lace *mantilla* to cover their head, like the ones you see in old Spanish movies. They kneel and pray and do the sign of the cross with a practised determination that seems to me very old-fashioned and even dangerously counter-revolutionary. I don't think they have ever heard about religion being the opium of the masses either.

Still, I must admit that it's very quiet and peaceful in here, almost like the perfect place for a siesta. It's nothing like outside, where it is noisy and where the sun shines and the sky is so blue and so bright that I swear your eyes hurt just from looking at it. So we sit here, not wanting to be here, listening to the priest talk about how good Catholics can enter the kingdom of God, which means nothing much to me but seems to have convinced the old ladies sitting right at the front near the altar.

The priest, Father Emerio, must be somewhere in his late

forties. He is not very tall but he looks strong, and has wavy black hair and a deep voice that you can hear everywhere in the church. My father thinks Father Emerio is all right. In approving tones he tells me that Father Emerio is not like other priests. He is a real Cuban who doesn't mind the occasional *tragito de rón*—a shot of rum—and is not afraid of defending himself with his fists, if necessary. He is no ordinary priest, my father adds. He fought in the Sierra Maestra mountains with Fidel! It's true!

At first I think my father must be confused: how can you have fought in the Sierra Maestra and be a priest? Didn't Fidel say that priests are counter-revolutionaries? But I will soon discover that my father is right. If you go into Father Emerio's office, which is in the house where he lives, attached to the side of the church, you can see the proof with your very own eyes, right there on his big desk: framed black and white photographs of someone who looks like a younger version of him standing next to Fidel and to other *barbudos*, I am sure, when they were all fighting against Batista in the mountains.

Sometime later, when I ask one of the women who helps out in church about the photographs, she tells me that Father Emerio was a chaplain with the rebels in the Sierra Maestra, in the days before Fidel discovered what Marx had to say about religion being the opium of the masses. You know, the woman who helps out in the church says, Father Emerio was such a good fighter in the Sierra Maestra, he was made a captain in the rebel army! By Fidel!

When I tell my friends at school about my discovery, they don't believe me, and frankly I don't blame them because I am still a little unsure about all this myself. Some of the kids in my class have their own stories about Father Emerio. They say he is a hypocrite because, you know, he has a *mujer*—a woman, a lover—and priests are not supposed to have lovers of any type because that, *chico*, is a big, big sin. And if he is such a good revolutionary and if he was a captain with the *barbudos* and if he knows Fidel, then tell me, how come he doesn't go to cut sugarcane on Sundays?

I think my friends have probably heard these stories from their own parents, but still I don't believe them. I have seen the photographs and I am beginning to think that Father Emerio is all right too. So when he suggests that my brother and I might want to become altar boys—*monaguillos*—we immediately say yes. I know deep down that this is going to look bad at school, especially since we will have to wear white robes at mass and stand around behind the altar pretending to be serious, but how can we say no to Father Emerio? He used to be a *barbudo* and if he thinks it's all right to be a *monaguillo*, then that's good enough for me. Besides, a couple of our neighbourhood friends, Jorgito and Pepitin, have now started coming to church too, probably because their mothers are not very good revolutionaries either, and they have probably been speaking to my mother. They are also going to be *monaguillos*.

After a time I begin to think that the smell of the incense is hypnotising me, just like Marx said it would, because slowly I start getting caught up in all this church business. As the Sundays roll on, I start to enjoy coming to mass, although of course there is no way I am going to let my mother know this, let alone my school friends. I start to understand a little bit more about the Pope and all the saints and what all the prayers mean and why we have to kneel and praise the Lord. To be truthful, I am still coming to terms with the idea of God being three people at once because it makes no sense to me at all, but I no longer mind having to sit here in my *monaguillos* robes listening to Father Emerio reading in his deep voice from the Book of Matthew or the Book of John—how can you tell which is which anyway? From where

I sit at the altar, I can smell the beeswax candles as they slowly melt, and hear the small choir as they sing another one of those hymns that ends up stuck in your brain for hours . . . *Que alegria cuando nos dijeron, vamos a la casa del Señor, Ya estan tocando nuestros pies, tus humbrales Jerusalem* . . . And you know, they sing some of the hymns with a hint of Cuban rhythm, which is funny because you can't help but tap your feet, right here in church.

Right after mass, once we have taken off our robes and helped Father Emerio pack up, a whole group of us run up the stairs at the back of the church to the big room on the top floor for our regular catechism class. This room has a small window from where, if you stand on the tip of your toes, you can see half of Banes, all the streets and the parks and my school. We are supposed to learn more about God from our catechism teacher but in reality we spend a lot of the time just playing around, sometimes imitating Father Emerio or the old ladies with their black *mantillas*, or just exploring the boxes that are stacked up neatly against the back wall, as if searching for treasure, which is exactly what we find one Sunday. A kind of treasure.

Inside one of the boxes, neatly folded, there are two dozen dress-up costumes like the ones they use in plays on television, made of shiny, silky, colourful fabrics that smell of another time. We can't believe our eyes. There is a John the Baptist costume, a Virgin Mary costume, costumes to dress up as the Three Wise Men, as one of the shepherds, or even as Mary Magdalene. But by far the most popular is the Roman centurion costume, because that costume comes with a sword and a helmet bearing bright red plumes, and eventually we get so rowdy and so noisy and start arguing so loudly about who is going to be the first to try on the Roman centurion costume—even the girls—that Father Emerio walks up the stairs and tells us, Children, I think it's time to go home. Church is over for the week.

When I tell my mother about these strange, foreign costumes, she explains that *antes del Triunfo* the church used to organise huge processions during Holy Week and every Christmas, right through the middle of Banes, stopping all traffic as if it was carnival time, and children from the parish would dress up as religious characters for the parade. Then, *despues del Triunfo*, when Fidel decided that religion was oppressing Cubans, it all stopped, she says. Religious processions are no longer allowed, not outside the church, anyway. Inside, you can pray all you want, and even ask God for anything you wish, but once you step out onto the streets that now belong to the People, there is no God.

Two of my best friends live just a few doors down from our house: Raulito and Fidelito. They are about the same age as my brother and me, we go to the same school, we go to the movies together, and we spend a lot of time playing together. I think Raulito was named after his father, Raul, while Fidelito, on the other hand, was named after Fidel, which wasn't at all uncommon back in 1959, according to my mother. The problem for Raulito and Fidelito is that their family's love affair with the *barbudos* was short-lived. They are now well-known *gusanos* in Banes, which may explain why Fidelito wants everyone to stop calling him Fidelito and call him by his middle name. He is not having much success.

I like their house, especially their backyard, which is nothing like my backyard. Theirs is big, grassy and has shady trees while ours has no grass and only the coconut tree in the far corner that is at war with my mother. Every now and then, when you least expect it, down comes a coconut, crashing onto the roof of the house or demolishing the clothesline again, driving my mother crazy so that she yells at my father, That tree has got to go! It will kill one of my boys one day! It has to go! And my father says, Yes, yes, it will go soon . . . But it will be years before the tree gets chopped down.

Apart from the big shady backyard, there is another reason my other friends and I like visiting Raulito and Fidelito. We like their parents too. Their father knows a lot about history and geography and he has lots of carpentry tools that he uses to make toys and all sorts of wooden gadgets for his sons, while their mother is always calm and her hair is always perfect. They have a television set that works and also, believe it or not, an American car that is probably about ten years old. It still shines in the sun as if it were brand new, though it doesn't get driven all that much because petrol is rationed. And the parents never, ever fight, at least not while I am there. They seem to be the perfect family.

When I get home from school today and tell my mother I am going to Raulito's house, she says, No, not today, and I can tell something is wrong. I have no idea what is going on but it doesn't take long for the news to get around: Raul, the father, has disappeared. He has been gone for two or three days, and no one has heard from him, which means only one thing—he has left the country illegally. The story we hear from our neighbours is that Raul and a handful of other men from Banes spent the past few weeks secretly building a raft of some sort somewhere near the coast, stowing provisions and waiting for the right moment to put out to sea and row all the way to Florida. I know this happens because we are always hearing stories about someone somewhere who had had enough of Fidel and packed the entire family onto some rickety raft they built in secret and attempted to make it across the water. Some make it and everyone in Banes knows someone who has managed to get to the other side alive and well, if a little sunburnt. And those lucky enough to make it to

El Norte, well, they are received with open arms by the Americans, according to one of my mother's friends. They are given piles of extra ham and cheese without having to queue, they get tender steaks for dinner every night, and a colour television set (yes, colour!), a new house with air conditioning and a pool, a new car and all the hairspray they want. They are the lucky ones.

But most of the stories we hear are of people who don't make it. Everyone knows of someone who knows someone who didn't make it. Everyone knows of someone who knows someone who either drowned on the crossing because of bad weather, or who got eaten by sharks. Or they got caught by the Cuban coast guard and sent back home and straight to prison because it's illegal to leave Cuba. It's bad enough being a *gusano*, but a *gusano* who tries to leave without permission and fails is the absolute worst, particularly in a small town like Banes. It's as though a big sign has been burnt into your forehead and the foreheads of all your brothers and sisters and your parents and your uncles and aunts and even your grandparents that says, I Am a Failed *Gusano*. Still, the stories of people trying to leave Cuba this way get told and retold and embellished by everyone in town, including my father, who listens to the ever more daring descriptions with what I assume to be a mixture of admiration and fear. *Esa gente sí que tienen cojones*, he says. Those people really have big balls. But I know there is no way in the world he would even consider taking his family out of Cuba that way. There is no way in the world my mother would agree anyway.

In our street, no one knows for sure what happened to Raul or to the others who left on the raft but everyone has a theory. Some of my friends are absolutely sure they were eaten by sharks. *Sí, sí, chico, los tiburones se los comieron*. The sharks ate them. Just like that. It will be days before my friends' family confirms, with a sense of relief but also apprehension, that Raul and the others were not eaten by sharks but did make it to Florida and that they are all fine. I am happy for my friends' father, who is now eating all that ham and cheese and driving a brand new car, but I can't help feeling sorry for Raulito and Fidelito because I know they miss their father a lot and because I know, like everyone else in our neighbourhood knows, that life is about to become a lot tougher for them.

★

It's official now: I am not going to Russia. Repeat, I am not going to Russia. And my mother is over the moon. For years she has lived with this fear, a fear that is never spoken about out loud but which is there, ever present, that at some stage the Revolution will take her boys away from her and send them either to a boarding school in Havana or, worse, to a boarding school in one of those cold, distant countries on the other side of the world that are now Cuba's best friends. Like Russia.

I think my mother is crazy to think the Revolution will take her children away to the Soviet Union so we can be taught how to become good communists. It will be years before I find out that she wasn't all that far wrong. Somewhere in Havana in the late 1960s there was a plan to do exactly that—select the best and brightest Cuban children and send them to be educated in Eastern Europe, whether their parents liked it or not. For some reason, the plan was never implemented.

The whole Russian thing came about because of a competition at my school to celebrate the anniversary of the birth of Vladimir Ilych Lenin. Nowadays we learn a lot about Vladimir Ilych Lenin at school because, as I am sure everyone knows, he is a great historic figure, an inspiration not just to the people of the Soviet Union but to people around the world, according to my teachers. Vladimir Ilych Lenin, we are told at school, is the reason we live in such a great country today, with free health care for all, and free schools, and no one begging on the streets. It's the reason why the smarter kids at school want to learn Russian too, which my friends tell me is a very difficult language to learn but it will become, for sure, the most important language when the entire world is communist. So, to celebrate Vladimir Ilych Lenin's birth date every school in the province has been asked to get their students to write a composition, which can be on any topic we choose but which I know should be patriotic. A good, patriotic, revolutionary composition—you can just tell that this is what they will be looking for. The student who writes the winning composition in the municipality gets to go to Russia, along with children from all the other municipalities in Cuba. It's quite a prize, especially for a boy from Banes who loves writing and loves compositions and who has barely been outside Banes, let alone outside Cuba.

It doesn't take me long to write my entry. It's a story about a group of children in Vietnam, which is another of those fraternal socialist countries we learn so much about at school. Every day on television, at school and in the paper, we learn about the heroic people of Vietnam fighting the imperialist Yankees, who are bombing their families and their schools and killing children with chemicals that burn your skin and destroy your face. I write about children in Vietnam who, after school, go about fighting the Americans, taking secret messages to grown-ups, building traps in the jungle with bamboo spikes, using whatever weapons they can find to shoot down planes with the initials USAF on the side. Except one day the children get caught in a bombing raid and one of them is killed by the Americans. Before he dies he tells his friends how they should turn his blood-soaked shirt into a flag—the red flag of North Vietnam. I am quite proud of my effort, although I am not sure whether it will be inventive enough to win the big prize. I can only hope.

Within days I get the news: I have won the competition in my school. I know because one of my teachers rushes up to me and tells me, although she makes me promise not to tell anyone until the official announcement is made. They must have told my mother too, because when I get home she is not happy at all and starts talking crazy stuff about how she isn't going to let her son go anywhere, let alone the Soviet Union. They will keep you there, she says, which I don't believe for a moment. No way, she keeps saying.

Tonight, however, we get a visit from Ibis, one of the Tavera sisters who live in the big house just across the street from us and who is also a teacher at my school. Ibis has come very quietly to bring the news my mother has been praying for: I am not going to Russia. Repeat, not going to Russia. There has been some mistake, she says. My composition didn't win after all.

At first I can't understand it. Sure, my mother is happy, but I am disappointed and then angry because I had already been told I had won first prize. I am sure of this and I can't understand why they would say I had won the prize and the trip to Russia and now I have not. It takes me a while to realise what Ibis is saying but eventually I get it: I am not going because—well, you know, my parents are not what you would call exemplary revolutionaries, are they? We are not *integrados*, which is the term everyone uses to refer to anyone who is a really, really good revolutionary.

In my mind I picture a room full of teachers discussing the revolutionary merits of my composition. Then, at the end, when they have decided that my composition is the best because it is, after all, about children in Vietnam who are fighting the imperialists, I imagine one of the teachers at the back giving a little cough and saying, Excuse me, *compañeros*, excuse me. Just hold on a second . . . This may be a very revolutionary composition but do you know that the boys' parents are . . . suspect? You know, his father never volunteers for *trabajo voluntario*, his mother owns a shop, which is a classic sign of petit bourgeois tendencies, and his aunt and uncle are *gusanos* who left Cuba for the United States.

I imagine the room going quiet and no one saying anything, and then, after a long pause, someone says, Yes, well, here is another excellent, revolutionary composition, stressing the word *revolutionary* to make sure that this time there is no mistake. Just like that, my prize, my trip to Moscow, is given to someone else, someone whose parents are much better revolutionaries than mine. So, I win second prize. It's a book about Vladimir Ilych Lenin, of course, with glossy colour illustrations of the Soviet leader standing heroically in the snow, looking serious as the wind lifts the side of his woollen coat, and pointing into the distance as if he is pointing the way to the communist future of the entire world, which is probably what the painter had in mind.

It's a nice book, you know, but it's not first prize. I am not happy. My mother is. I will never get to Russia.

12 · ¡CHE LIVES!

Che is dead. The news has just come in and it has come from *El Maxímo Líder*. That's how important the news must be. Ernesto Guevara has been killed, Fidel said on television and radio, adding that Che was murdered by the CIA somewhere in Bolivia, which I know is a poor country in South America. Che was killed while fighting the Americans and their lackeys in the Bolivian army, Fidel said, and now all of Cuba is in mourning for three days to honour the man who is to be known from now on as *El Guerrillero Heroico*, or The Heroic Guerrilla.

Frankly, I am not too sure what all the fuss is about. Like every school child in Cuba, I know who Che is because we have been taught how Che was the *comandante* in charge of the rebels during the great Battle of Santa Clara, which was the turning point in the fighting by the *barbudos* against Fulgencio Batista back in 1958. I also know that later, *despues del Triunfo*, Fidel made Che a senior minister in charge of industry in the new Revolutionary Government and even sent him to Russia to get some ideas about how to run a good communist economy.

Even now, you sometimes come across Cuban revolutionary *pesos* signed by Che when he was also head of the central bank back in the early days. But we haven't heard about Che for a long time because at least two or three years ago he just disappeared from public view.

No one seemed to know where he was but that isn't all that strange in Cuba. Important people, like ministers and *comandantes* in the Revolutionary Armed Forces and Communist Party leaders even, can disappear from television or from the newsreels without warning, and you never really know why—or if they are coming back. Then, in October 1965, Fidel said on television that Che had left Cuba for good and moved to Africa looking for *nuevos campos de batallas*—new battlefields against the imperialists. No one has heard anything about Che since then, so you can see why some people are a little surprised by Fidel's announcement that Che has been killed in battle. Not in Africa but in Bolivia.

At the end of the three-day mourning period, Fidel gives another big speech and you can tell it's not going to be a happy speech because *El Maxímo Líder* looks and sounds as if he is tired, his hair is all over the place and his face is covered in sweat—and that is even before he starts. There are about a million people in the Plaza de la Revolución, the big square in Havana where all the major rallies against the Americans are held, and all the Cuban flags are at half mast. To one side of Fidel up on the podium there is a huge photograph of Che, as tall as a ten-storey apartment block, looking heroic and revolutionary. Fidel says that while Che has died, he is still alive. One of my neighbourhood friends says this means Che is alive and will never die, no matter what the CIA does, because he is like one of those zombies you see in movies. I am sure he is only joking.

The family of another of my neighbourhood friends have their own theories about the death of Che—they have told him that they think Fidel is to blame. They think that Che was sent to South America by Fidel to get rid of him because he was becoming too much trouble for Fidel and for Fidel's brother Raul. So they sent him away to a place where the CIA could get at him and kill him. I know my friend's family are not communists—I think they may be *gusanos*—but I don't know where they get these crazy, counter-revolutionary ideas from. I think they are looking for trouble, but when I tell my father what I have been told he says, to my surprise, that he also thinks Fidel had something to do with Che's death. He says a lot of people in Cuba think the same way.

The thing about Che dying is that now there is nothing on television, on the radio or at the cinema but stories about Che. Even at school we have assemblies and meetings where we spend almost all day talking about Che and what a great example he is to Cuban children. At the end of all these meetings, right after we stand up to sing the national anthem—and sometimes, too, the 'Internationale'—we now say in a loud voice, *¡Seremos como el Che!* We will be like Che. Which means we will be true revolutionaries, not interested in money or material things, ready to fight the imperialists anywhere in the world. I have no problem being like Che because I know he was a revolutionary hero and it all sounds like dangerous fun, but I wish we didn't have to spend our time talking about Che so we could get back to normal, seeing movies at the cinema and listening to music on the radio again.

Even though, like all my classmates, I keep saying that I want to grow up to be just like Che, I still don't really understand what it means. In October 1967 I have no idea that nearly forty years later, photographs of Che in his trademark black beret will be plastered on expensive designer t-shirts, or that a film about his youth would be made not in Cuba, but in a capitalist country by capitalist film-makers. And the film would make money—the very thing Che wanted to do away with.

That is all way in the future, though. Right now I am at school listening to yet another reading of Che's diary in Bolivia. This happens every day. Che's diary of his time in Bolivia has been turned into a book, which has been published in record time in Cuba and then distributed to every Cuban workplace and every Cuban school and every Cuban library, so we can all learn from his revolutionary example. Every day at some time or other, we get an entry from Che's diary in Bolivia read to us in class and while we may not be literary experts, my friends and I agree that the diaries are pretty heavy going. Except for the bits about fighting the Bolivian army there is not much in there that would make me or my friends want to fly out to the jungles of South America to spread revolution, probably because we can't follow what Che is trying to say. Still, we all sit quietly at our desks listening to the teacher read on and on and on, because if you say you don't want to grow up to be just like Che, you may have some explaining to do.

In Cuba we have lots of revolutionary heroes like Che. All of them are dead. There is Frank Pais and Antonio Mella and Abel Santamaria, but everyone's favourite seems to be Camilo Cienfuegos, who was a commander in the rebel army. As feared, able and famous as Fidel, he commanded the battalions that secured much of eastern Cuba, which made him into a very popular figure. In all those pictures of Fidel travelling through the island in a convoy of trucks and Cadillacs with long fins on their way to Havana in January 1959, there is Camilo. He is always standing next to Fidel, his beard is longer than anyone else's, he wears what seems like a big cowboy hat tilted back just a tad like in the western movies, and he is always smiling. Even his eyes smile. My mother says the girls were big Camilo fans, hinting that at the start of the Revolution most Cuban women found him *muy buen mozo*, which is what Cuban women say when they mean someone is a good looker.

I know that what makes the Camilo story so interesting, at least for me, is not that he was a hero in life but that he became a hero in death, which is also a very Cuban kind of thing. It's a story every Cuban school child also knows off by heart: Camilo died on 25 October 1959, just months after entering Havana with Fidel as a conquering hero. He was on his way back to Havana from the province of Camaguey when the small plane he was flying in mysteriously disappeared over the Caribbean, his body never to be recovered. And so, every 25 October, every school in Cuba marks the death of smiling, hat-wearing, battle-weary Camilo. My school travels to one of the beaches near Banes to listen to revolutionary speeches, sing the national anthem and throw flowers into the sea. To remember Camilo.

What no one talks about or even mentions during the revolutionary speeches and the singing and the flower throwing is that when Camilo's light plane disappeared, he was on his way back from a mission he undertook on the express orders of Fidel—to arrest another revolutionary commander, Huber Matos, who a few days earlier had announced he would be resigning as military commander of Camaguey province, along with a dozen other *barbudos*, because he was unhappy with the rising influence of communists in the Revolutionary Government. According to my father's version of the story, Fidel was furious and ordered Camilo to fly to Camaguey at once, arrest Matos and charge him with treason, which Camilo apparently did reluctantly. Matos would be sentenced to twenty years in prison, which he dutifully served until 1989, when he was finally released and allowed to leave Cuba with his family for the United States.

My father says that Camilo, who was a good middle class boy from a good, Catholic middle class home, agreed with Huber Matos and had told Fidel that he, too, was quitting, which of course would have been a huge embarrassment for the Revolution. And so, my father says, Fidel ensured that Camilo never made it back to Havana alive. That's what really happened, he says. And that, he adds, is what has happened to Che too!

I am not sure. I am beginning to suspect my father has a counter-revolutionary explanation for just about everything, which is not a great example at all for a boy who wants to grow up to be just like Che!

13 · GIANT PINEAPPLES AND OTHER SOCIALIST MIRACLES

In the cinema newsreel there is footage of Fidel in his green uniform, which is all he ever seems to wear, holding two pineapples. But these are not ordinary pineapples. These are huge. They are as big as oversized watermelons and Fidel is saying that these are the type of pineapples revolutionary scientists have developed in Cuba using the latest socialist technology. They are huge pineapples and they are supposed to be tastier and meatier and a lot more juicy than ordinary, capitalist pineapples.

As he speaks, Fidel is surrounded by the scientists in white coats and by the farmers who have come up with what I am sure are the biggest pineapples in the entire world. He says the pineapples are only in the development stage but soon enough they will be growing all over Cuba so that every family in the country can eat as much pineapple as they want. There will be so many giant pineapples we will export them all over the world. This is what the Revolution can do, *El Maximo Lider* says, holding the two giant pineapples up for the cameras while everyone around him nods in approval and applauds.

I think it's great that Cuba now has the world's biggest and best pineapples, because this will show those Yankees what we revolutionary Cubans can do by working hard. We are good at coming up with great ideas like this, we Cubans. Mind you, I know this isn't going to impress my father. It seems as if there is nothing Fidel can do that will impress him nowadays. And I know that when I tell my mother, she will say something like, We haven't seen pineapples in the shops since 1960, which is true, of course, but does she have to be so counter-revolutionary?

I don't care. I may not be allowed to join the communist pioneers but I am still a proud little Cuban and I am very proud that the Revolution has managed to grow giant pineapples, so I tell them what I saw at the cinema and, sure enough, they are not impressed. My mother says, We haven't even seen normal sized pineapples in the shops for years! My father then says, I hope this giant pineapple is not like the giant strawberries Fidel was talking about last year.

Now, that comes as a shock. Giant strawberries? This is something entirely new to me. Giant pineapples, yes, I know about them, but giant strawberries? What are these giant strawberries I have never heard about? I know that when Fidel gave a speech to the Federation of Cuban Women he promised them giant cows that would provide so much milk everyone in Cuba would be drinking milk at breakfast, lunch and even dinner. In fact, there would be so much milk from the giant cows we would be selling milk to the Americans! I can just picture those embarrassed Americans having to drink Cuban milk! And yes, I know that Fidel also said Cuba would soon be producing more brie cheese and better quality brie cheese than the Europeans, but I had never, ever heard about the giant tropical strawberries. Anyway, it's too late in the day to start asking my father. I have school tomorrow and I decide instead to cut my losses and go to bed where, of course, I dream of giant strawberries that start chasing me through the house until I wake up in a panic, crying out for my *mami*.

★

In Banes, no one talks about the past. Or at least not in a good way. In public, everyone talks about how bad things were *antes del Triunfo*, before Fidel came down from the mountains with his beard and his guns and kicked out Batista and his corrupt politicians, the American Mafia and the rich landowners who exploited the poor workers. There is even a song about it, a *guaracha* they used to play on the radio all the time, titled, *Llego el Comandante y mandó a parar*, which translates as, Fidel arrived and put a stop to all that. There are lots of revolutionary songs like that in Cuba. We get those stories all the time at school and on television and in the papers because that is the history of Cuba. It will be many years before I recognise that this is a heavily edited version of the history of Cuba, but even at my age I suspect there must be another side to the story because I have heard my mother's aunts, who are so old they all have white hair, talk about the good old days in Banes. That's what they say—the good old days in Banes.

One of my mother's aunts, Juana, who is short and wiry and always smoking and coughing, usually at the same time, tells me that there was a time when there was plenty of money to go around in the town and lots of places in which to spend all that money. It was a time, she says with a wink, when everyone in Banes was a supporter of Batista because, after all, Batista was a Banes boy. Which is news to me.

If you ask her, Aunt Juana will tell you that Batista was born just outside the town in 1901, and that his parents were very

111

poor and of mixed race—they had some white, some black and even some Chinese blood, which meant that he was a *mulato*. And a clever one, too, she says, raising one of her eyebrows. He left Banes in 1921 to join the army and within a few years he had been promoted to a military stenographer with the rank of sergeant. He was attached to the Army Supreme Command, which wasn't bad for a poor kid from a small town in a corner of Oriente province.

Batista was popular and crafty and ambitious, and in 1933 he became involved in a rebellion that was to topple the dictator of the day, Gerardo Machado. A year later, Batista was at it again. He led what became known as the Revolution of the Sergeants, a revolt against the temporary government that had proved to be highly inefficient and unpopular. From that moment on, Batista, who had been promoted to head of the army, became a major political figure in Cuba. Because he was from peasant stock one of his many nicknames was *El Guajirito de Banes*, the Little Peasant Boy from Banes, which wasn't meant to be much of a compliment. If you believe Aunt Juana, many people in Banes were very happy to be supporters of his—*batistianos*—even though, she says, Batista was no saint—*no era un santo*—and imprisoned and tortured anyone who opposed him.

When he was the strongman of Cuba, Batista would regularly visit Banes. Wearing an immaculate suit, his friends and supporters trailing behind him, he would shower everyone with money, says Aunt Juana. It wasn't his money, of course, but government money which in effect was the same thing. He would visit his old home town and make speeches and have a big dinner with the most important people in town at the old Club Banes, which used to be the rich people's club but which now belongs to the People—or, more accurately, to the People who run the Communist Party in Banes. Every time Batista visited he left money behind to build something new, like a hospital, or to pave some streets or the new big road that takes you to the resort of Guardalavaca which, according to my father, was good news for local tourist operators because it meant Guardalavaca became the second best known beach in the whole of Cuba. But now, says Aunt Juana, no one in Banes admits to ever having been a *batistiano*. Now no one talks about Batista in public, except to say what a tyrant he was.

Then again, no one in Banes talks about the times Fidel also used to visit the town. *El Maxímo Líder* was born only about one hundred kilometres away in an area called Biran, where his father owned a huge sugarcane plantation. Fidel even married a Banes girl he had met at university, Mirta Diaz Balart, whose family was one of the best known and most powerful in town— they worked for the United Fruit Company and, needless to say, were prominent supporters of Batista. The young couple married in the local church, the same church where my brother and I attend mass, and Aunt Juana tells me it was quite a wedding, with lots of rich people attending and half the town coming out to see the newlyweds. It was big news in the local paper, too, and everyone talked about the wedding for many days. Fidel and Mirta had a baby, Fidelito, but it wasn't long before the marriage collapsed and Mirta and her family left for Miami. Nowadays, of course, no one talks about it, not in the papers, nor on television or radio, and certainly not on the streets of Banes. Strange town.

My uncle Tony, who is my mother's brother, is visiting Banes. He comes to Banes a couple of times a year to see his sisters and, especially, to see my cousin Tonito, his son from his first marriage, to my aunt Anarda. They are now divorced, but my uncle and Tonito, who is a year older than me, remain close, which means that when he comes to Banes not only do we get to spend time with my cousin but also with my uncle.

My uncle Tony is tall, handsome in a Cuban kind of way and, as far as I can see, the most worldly of all my uncles. Unlike my parents, he reads lots of books and he enjoys talking about things that don't normally get talked about around our dinner table, like history, which is, you may have gathered, my favourite subject at school. The other thing that sets my uncle Tony apart from the rest of the family—and in fact from most other Cubans—is that he gets to travel overseas, without having to wait years for Fidel's permission. I never know exactly what his job title is or what the job entails, but without fail my uncle goes away every year to fraternal countries in Eastern Europe and even to friendly capitalist countries like Spain and France. I think he has even been to Italy, and you don't get more exotic than Italy when you come from Banes.

My uncle is the one member of the family everyone seems to turn to when they need help, because he knows exactly what to do and whom to talk to to get things sorted out. Apparently that is the way it has always been, according to my mother, even when he was younger. He is the Mister Fix-it, and I can tell that my mother and all my aunts worship the ground he walks on. When he visits he never talks about politics, even though I assume he is a member of the Communist Party, as those really important jobs—the ones where you are allowed to travel overseas—are normally open only to members of the Party. I think the fact that he doesn't talk about politics is one of the reasons my father gets along so well with him, even though my father is not a communist. Or even a half-decent socialist.

Every time my uncle comes to Banes, he bring presents.

Sometimes they are small presents, sometimes they are more substantial, but it doesn't matter much because presents of any type are rare in Banes, especially if they are presents from overseas. Even the smallest present from overseas feels like a window opening onto the outside, a window that exposes an impressionable child to a very different and unattainable world. This time my uncle Tony has brought chocolates from somewhere in Hungary, some chewing gum, a book for me from Spain, and a cake that I hope he picked up on his way into Banes when the bus stopped somewhere in Camaguey province, as I can't imagine the cake making it all the way from Europe.

Even better than all that, my uncle has brought my brother and me a pullover each from Europe. These are not ordinary socialist pullovers, either. They are soft to touch and they seem like the most sophisticated and luxurious clothing we have ever come across, which they probably are. Even the smell is so non-Cuban. There is just one problem—they are woollen pullovers, which means we are wearing them now in the middle of a Cuban summer and as soon as we put them on, we start to sweat and get itchy and uncomfortable. But they look so good, so foreign, that I don't care, so I wear my new pullover for the rest of the day, until my mother intervenes and insists I take it off and wait for it to get cool, which will be a long wait because it will be months before it is winter in Cuba, and even then it won't be very cold at all, at least not in Banes. Parents can be so unfair.

My uncle Tony has also brought some presents for my teenage cousin July: a new record which I assume he must have bought somewhere in England, though in reality he could have bought it almost anywhere in capitalist Europe, or even in Yugoslavia, which my father says is almost like a capitalist country. It's a Beatles record and my cousin couldn't be happier. I have never seen her quite as pleased with herself as she plays it again and again on her record player. I don't know much about The Beatles because as far as I can recall I have never heard their music or even their name on the radio. But my cousin obviously has because she is thrilled.

It's not difficult to see why: the music is catchy and exotic. And you can dance to this music, which is more than I can say for those protest songs and *Nueva Trova* music they play on the radio almost all the time now. Instead of *guarachas* and *boleros* and *rumbas*, all you get on radio are protest songs. All of my friends, sophisticated critics that we are, agree that protest songs may be revolutionary but they are also boring, and who in their right mind wants to dance to a song about some poor *campesino* family in Guatemala that are being exploited, maimed or murdered by bloodthirsty Yankees? They are not the type of songs you can dance to even if you wanted to. They are nothing like the old *boleros* my mother sometimes hums when she is doing the ironing, like *Bésame Mucho* or *Solamente una Vez*, which are sad songs, sure, but you can still dance to them, moving slowly and holding your partner really close, which my mother says is like dancing on top of a single brick—*bailando en un ladrillito*.

I love my cousin July, and not just because she owns what is probably the only record of The Beatles in Banes. I wish I had a record of The Beatles, so I could show it off to my school friends even if we don't own a record player. But that's the thing about my cousin—she is always one step ahead. She is old enough to go to films that I cannot see, and worldly enough to spend hours talking to her friends, who are all loud like she is, about things I don't understand, like boys and make-up. It explains why she knew all about The Beatles even though we never get to hear them on the radio because they have long hair and in Cuba you are not allowed to have long hair.

A friend of my cousin says The Beatles are banned from

Cuban radio because they are not considered a good revolutionary example. They are considered a bad influence on teenagers, who will be seduced into capitalism and decadence by 'I Want to Hold Your Hand' and 'Love Me Do'. Instead of volunteering to cut sugarcane or attending meetings to discuss Marx, young Cubans who listen to The Beatles will be corrupted and spend their time sitting around doing nothing, letting their hair grow long and reading subversive, capitalist books. All of which will make me wonder, years later, what was my uncle Tony thinking? What was he trying to say when he brought back the Beatles record for my cousin July?

14 · IN EVERY *BARRIO*, REVOLUTION

Every neighbourhood in Cuba, whether you live in a big city like Havana or a small, forgotten town like Banes, has its own Committee for the Defence of the Revolution, known to everyone as the CDR or *el Comite*. Or sometimes *los chivatos*, which is Cuban slang for someone who snitches. A dobber. Of course, you never call them that in public unless you are dumb or looking for trouble and, to be honest, there are plenty of other ways to get into trouble in Cuba without having to bother the hardworking revolutionaries of the local CDR.

In our neighbourhood, like in all others, *el Comite* rules supreme. As the name implies, they were originally set up in 1960 to defend the Revolution. Neighbours would join to help patrol the local streets at night, keeping an eye on anyone stupid enough to attempt to plant a bomb or paint anti-Castro slogans on the walls, which happened every now and then in the first year or so after *el Triunfo*. Then the CDRs were used to organise whole streets of volunteers to go and cut sugarcane on Sundays, or to join huge marches to protest against those Yankees who wanted to kill Fidel with exploding cigars. But in time, *el Comite* has become much more than that, as every Cuban knows.

Nothing gets done without *el Comite* having a say. For instance, if you want to complain about dogs barking late into the night, you go to *el Comite*. If you want someone to come and help you paint your house, you go and talk to *el Comite*, or if you are having problems at home with your kids, well, you go to *el Comite* too, and someone there will sit you down in a hard, straight-backed wooden chair and give you a little explanation about why you should obey your mother and work hard and study hard and learn how to use a rifle so you can defend the Revolution. If you want to travel to Havana it's wise to check with *el Comite* first since you will need permission to take time off work and to get a bus ticket. Need to vaccinate your baby? The CDR will arrange it for you. Same if you are thinking of changing jobs which, in reality, is almost impossible in Cuba.

The CDR in our neighbourhood organises street parties some Saturdays, which is good because it means everyone comes into the balmy Caribbean night, the adults to gossip with their neighbours and the kids to run around on bikes, and as the breeze from the coast starts to pick up a little, someone will bring out a radio and there will be music playing and before you know it, everyone will be dancing, which is the most Cuban thing you can do. And then, the next morning, it's back to normal.

A lot of the time you don't have to tell *el Comite* anything—they know even before you do. That's how good they are. They come to your house and check your possessions if you are a *gusano* who has applied to leave the country. They come to your house and ask you why you had so many visitors last night, and what they were doing until so late. They knock on your door and ask you to turn the music down because, *compañero*, we are all going on volunteer work to cut sugarcane tomorrow morning on the dot of five—you are coming, aren't you? And the CDR people always know all the gossip in the neighbourhood—who is sleeping with whom, which marriage is on the rocks, who is having an abortion. It's that kind of organisation and, not surprisingly, it tends to attract and nurture the nosiest people in every neighbourhood, though of course they don't think they are nosey. They are just good revolutionaries doing their socialist duty.

It's the same if you want to snitch on one of your neighbours—or on your parents. You go to the woman from *el Comite* and tell her that your parents are saying things they shouldn't about Fidel, and then she will do *her* revolutionary duty and tell the police and then, before you know it, there is a *miliciano* on the doorstep asking questions, which is never a good thing. But the revolutionary task the CDR enjoys above all others is keeping an eye on what the newspaper calls anti-social elements, which means they spend a lot of their time keeping tabs on teenagers with long hair who listen to capitalist music, and on anyone they think may be a homosexual. And we all know from school that homosexuals—known as *maricones* in Cuba, or sometimes *mariquitas*—are the most dangerous and evil counter-revolutionaries of all, with the exception of *gusanos*, of course, or *gusanos* who also happen to be *maricones*.

In our neighbourhood the CDR is headed by a woman who lives a few houses up from us, just around the corner. I don't really know—no one does—how she was selected or by whom, but naturally she is *de los duros*—a hardline communist—which may explain why we refer to her as *La Compañera*. My mother says that before her elevation, *La Compañera* was someone with whom you exchanged polite, neighbourly conversation every now and then but no more. Since *el Triunfo*, though, she has become a very important person in our little corner of the world.

She always wears her militia uniform and she loves to gossip with the neighbours, or at least those neighbours she considers ideologically committed. It's not that she is rude to my parents, nothing like that, but you know she is keeping an eye on us. Which scares me, because I know very well that my parents are not good revolutionaries. You see, my father never puts his name down for volunteer work in the sugarcane fields, saying he works hard enough through the week without having to give up his Sundays as well. Besides, he says, half the time is spent not cutting sugarcane at all but listening to speeches by some local Communist Party leader about how terrific things are in Cuba— *¡vamos bien!*—and how much, much better they could be if only everyone worked a little bit harder and the Americans stopped planning to invade the island. There are other people in the neighbourhood who never put their names down for volunteer work either, despite the disapproving looks of the woman boss from the CDR, but it's not really something you brag about. You just pretend you are busy with something else.

The truth is, though, that if you want to get anywhere in Cuba you need to do volunteer work, or at least you have to be seen to be doing volunteer work, because whether you do or not is the type of detail that goes straight into your personal files: the *expediente laboral* if you are a working-age adult, or the *expediente escolar* if, like me, you are at school. Everything you do and everything you say goes into your personal files, including anything you may have said that someone may have misinterpreted as being disloyal to the Revolution, which is why my mother always tells us to be careful about what we say: *Ten cuidado con lo que dices, niño.*

Even school children understand how important the *expediente* is because it is used time and again to decide your future, like whether you are going to go to university or not when you finish school. A revolutionary *expediente* is essential if you want to join the Communist Youth Union, known as La Juventud, which is the first step to becoming a real communist, a member of the Communist Party, which in turn is the first step to gaining access to special shops in Havana where, I have it on good authority, you can buy ham and cheese and chewing gum and other stuff that you can never find in the local *bodega*, no matter how long or how often you queue. Of course, you need an exemplary *expediente* if you want to be given a Russian Lada car at work or permission to join a Cuban delegation travelling overseas, which is by far and away the most sought-after prize of all, even if you are only allowed to visit Bucharest and even if you are never, ever allowed to take any other member of your family with you.

The worst thing about the *expediente* is that you never really know what it says because you never get to see it, even if you ask politely. You know they have written things about you in the file but you don't ever find out what. You just hope it's all good. If it's all bad, you will eventually find out.

★

We are sitting in the Teatro Hernández, my brother and I and a few of our friends from the neighbourhood. It's just another night in Banes except we are pretty excited because we have all heard that the *Fantomas* sequel we are about to watch, *Fantomas se desencadena*, is supposed to be even better than the first film, which we watched some months ago. *Fantomas* is big in Cuba, and not just with children my age. It's weird, of course, because nothing could be further from the reality of revolutionary Cuba than one of these French films starring French actor Jean Marais, who has become, as you might expect, the most popular actor in all of Cuba. He plays Fandor, a sophisticated jewel thief who spends his time stealing from fashionable apartments in Paris, and then fleeing the police in magical cars that turn into airplanes.

The films have been a huge success right across Cuba. Now when my friends and I talk about someone who is good at escaping we call him Fantomas, that's how popular the films are. I don't really know why this should be the case but I imagine it's because what's up there on the screen is so far removed from our daily lives. Fantomas is always attending lavish parties in elegant palaces somewhere in the countryside, or in Paris in some big, big apartment, much bigger than the ones I saw in Havana. Up there on the screen the women all look like magazine models and they wear shiny, expensive clothes and huge diamonds made for stealing. They are always jumping in and out of those long limousines that no boy in this cinema—no boy in Banes—is ever likely to see in real life. I think that's why the cinema is always full when *Fantomas* films are shown. It's funny of course, because they are not very revolutionary films at all.

There are two cinemas in Banes: the Hernández, which is just at the end of our street, and at the other end of town, diagonally across from the Catholic church, the Heredia, where they show the Sunday matinees I no longer get to see because I am in the church. We go to the Hernández almost every night because it's the closest. We don't have a television set so it's the next best alternative. Besides, it's cheap and is one of the few things in Cuba that isn't rationed, so you can go as many times as you want. Mind you, it's very much hit and miss. Movies change every night, except for really popular films like *Fantomas*, which are shown two or even three nights in a row, but never longer than three nights because by then just about everyone in town would have seen it. The more popular the film, the longer it will run, which is another way of saying that Russian movies—of which there are lots—never get shown a second night.

Sometimes everyone in the family goes to the Hernández but most nights it's just my brother and me and our friends from the neighbourhood. Right after dinner we meet in the middle of the street and then walk down to the cinema which, like almost every other public building in Cuba that used to be owned by capitalists, has had its name changed. It is now called the Teatro Hanoi, in honour of the heroic Vietnamese people. Every time I walk into the foyer of the *teatro*, I wonder who had the job of coming up with the new revolutionary names, because that person must be very, very busy. Whoever came up with the new revolutionary name of Hanoi was very clever, though, since it means they didn't have to change the embroidered T and H on the curtains at the front. Of course, everyone in Banes still calls it the Hernández.

Teenagers love the Hernández, which is newer but more intimate than the Teatro Heredia. They sit right at the back and, like teenagers anywhere else, they kiss and do who-knows-what-else under the cover of darkness while younger kids like my brother and me and our friends sit in the middle, making silly noises like we are kissing until the lights dim and the projector high above the audience starts to roll noisily. Sometimes, if the film is boring, we start throwing paper planes at the teenagers kissing at the back and then someone will come out and tell us to stop or we will be thrown out.

To be honest, being thrown out is not such a bad option some nights, especially on nights when, instead of an old American western or some French musketeer film, they show one of those Russian films that can send you to sleep. Most of the Russian films are in black and white and have subtitles but that is not the problem—my friends and I don't mind black and white films with subtitles from Japan, like the samurai stories starring Toshiro Mifune, who almost overnight has become as popular among my friends in Banes as Jean Marais. As far as I can see, using all the critical faculties of a prepubescent boy in unsophisticated Banes, the problem with the Soviet films is that they are set in a world where everyone is poor or hungry and very unhappy. They are what my aunt Nidia would call depressing—*deprimente*—or dreary. Unlike *Fantomas*.

It's strange what makes it onto the screen. Fidel says capitalists are bad and decadent and want to destroy the Revolution, but it seems that many of the films we see at night are from capitalist countries, including old American films that have been pirated, dubbed and, in theory at least, carefully vetted for subliminal anti-revolutionary messages. Even more weird is the number of films we see from capitalist countries in Europe: comedies from England like *Doctor in Clover* and Morecambe and Wise, and French action films with Jean Paul Belmondo, in which men with guns are always driving fast cars and kissing beautiful French women on the lips. There is nothing very revolutionary about these films, you can tell, and yet they have been approved as suitable.

By far the most popular films are the soapy Spanish musicals and melodramas featuring famous film stars like Sarita Montiel, like *El Ultimo Cuple* or *La Violetera*, which always tell the same story about a poor girl from the country who arrives in the big city, starts off in modest cleaning jobs and then, using her musical talents, extreme good looks and her poise, becomes a major singing sensation or a movie star. It's not what you'd call an exemplary socialist tale, I am sure, but my mother loves these films as do my aunts and our neighbours and almost every other woman in Cuba. One of my aunts says these are the films loved by Franco, the Spanish dictator. She is right. But it's only years later that I realise how peculiar it is that the Spanish films that get the okay from the anti-communist censors in 1960s Spain are the same films that get the go-ahead from communist censors in 1960s Cuba.

★

There are not too many books in our house. My parents are not great readers, which my mother says is the result of her never having gone to secondary school—few girls of her age and class would have done so in a town like Banes when she was growing up. Not that there is a shortage of books in revolutionary Cuba. It's just that the choice is a little limited.

I walk into *La Marquesita*, which is the biggest of the stationery and book shops in Banes, and you can see that there are plenty of books on the shelves. Most of them have been written by Fidel or about Fidel, or are about how bad things were before Fidel. For just a few cents you can buy books about Che, *El Guerrillero Heroico*, as he has become universally known since his death in Bolivia, and books by Che, including his thoughts on guerrilla warfare, which we must all study at school but which everyone agrees is the dullest book of the lot.

Then there are books about the Glorious October Revolution, and plenty of Russian biographies of Vladimir Ilych Lenin, which you can buy for next to nothing. They are not fancy books—the covers are dull and the pages inside are badly glued together, so that they come apart almost as soon as you walk out of the shop. This is not a bad thing since by the time you get home with your Russian tome of Lenin's *What Is to Be Done* you can just make a hole through the loose pages and pin them up next to the toilet bowl for when you run out of toilet paper. I know, I know: it's not a very revolutionary thing to do but, believe me, even communists need toilet paper.

I have found that the best place for books in Banes is the municipal library, which is housed in a modern building in one of the main streets not far from our house. I feel right at home in there, sitting at one of the long tables in the middle of the room. The lights are bright and it's so quiet it is almost un-Cuban, and the lady behind the counter looks stern at first but later she smiles at me every time I walk in, as if secretly welcoming another convert into her little world of reading. It's as though I have found the perfect place and some nights I stay until closing time because it's so much nicer and quieter than home.

And once you make friends with the librarian, she will always alert you when new books arrive from Havana, especially books from overseas. It's in here that I discover the Tintin books, the fantastically rich and complex comics by the Belgian cartoonist Hergé, which the librarian says, in almost reverential tones, have been imported from Spain, as if explaining why the pages in these colourful books are so much thicker and more luxurious than the Russian-printed biographies of Lenin and Engels. And here I also discover Huckleberry Finn, published and printed in Spain although everyone knows it is an American story and this in itself is strange—an American story in the Banes municipal library.

I soon realise that these Spanish-printed books are the jewels in the library's collection, speaking as they do of an impossibly distant world in which the pages of books are very white, very shiny and smell and feel very expensive. That is why you can read these books in here for as long as you want—as I do—but you can't borrow many of them. I also realise in the way boys sometimes do that what makes the Tintin books so attractive to me is not just the quality of the paper and the colour of the illustrations and the fact that these books have travelled all the way from a distant country—a capitalist country, no less. It's the fact that if they have any political message to impart, it totally eludes me. They are just fun to read. In revolutionary Cuba, that is quite a rarity.

15 · THOSE BULGARIAN GIRLS

The Bulgarians have arrived. Two of them. Sisters. If I were a little older I would say I am smitten by them. Totally. Love at first sight. But because I am still a boy and girls remain something of a mystery, although it won't be for long now, all I feel is absolute wonder at these two exotic foreigners who have arrived at our school.

Their arrival is the biggest news at school since . . . well, since no one knows when. They are here, in my class, as part of some sort of student exchange program between Cuba and other communist countries, although I am not sure how it came about or who organised such an exchange since, as far as I can tell, none of my school friends in Banes has been invited to spend time in a Bulgarian school. It doesn't matter at all. Since *el Triunfo*, we don't get too many foreigners making the long trip from Havana to Banes—unless you count the Russian technicians that used to be here some years ago when the Americans and the Soviets were fighting over nuclear missiles. Even at carnival time, the musicians who come to Banes to perform are all Cubans. Foreign musicians

129

like Massiel, who is the most popular Spanish singer in Cuba, or the Italian Rita Pavone, who is also very famous, spend time only in Havana and never, ever travel further east than Varadero beach. Perhaps they don't have time or perhaps they don't think there is much to see.

I am told that our Bulgarian visitors are here for three months, and within days, just like that, they have turned our school upside down. They both have blonde hair that they comb into a plait finished off with one of those red silk ribbons I have seen girl pioneers wear while marching or travelling in trolley cars in Russian documentaries. They have blue eyes and skin that looks so soft and so white, almost like milk, you just know the girls will have to stay out of the Cuban sun or they will turn pink like the inside of a watermelon. They look like what I imagine a snow queen to look like, so different to the Cuban girls in my class, whose skin is much darker, whose eyes are the colour of almonds and who would look totally out of place anywhere near the snow.

The Bulgarian girls look fragile too, and a little confused, probably from all the attention they are getting, not just in our classroom but whenever they venture out of class into the cement playground; or when they go out in town and people whisper and point, because by now everyone knows they are *las niñas bulgaras* and everyone waves and says something nice in Spanish and the girls wave back, trying to smile but really looking totally terrified.

The sisters are staying with a girl in our class whose family live in a house right on General Marrero Street, but who is not and has never been one of my friends at school. I can't understand why she has been picked for such an honour, especially since everyone knows her parents aren't even members of the Communist Party. I suspect she doesn't like me at all because no matter how hard I try to ingratiate myself with her so that I can speak to the Bulgarian sisters, she just pushes past me, ignoring my attempts—my lame attempts, I know—to be her friend. It probably serves me right, I think, because until now I have never made the slightest effort to be friends. I don't think she ever had too many friends, really, but that has all changed now that she is hosting the Bulgarian sisters. Now, her social standing at school has shot sky-high. She is the queen of the playground and I hate her.

The Bulgarian sisters speak only a little Spanish but somehow they manage to get themselves understood by the rest of the class, which isn't surprising since we are all so eager, desperate, to befriend them. When I get the chance, I speak to them in halting Spanish, speaking really slowly, as if that is going to make it easier for them to understand what I say. They smile at me and then move back to the girl from General Marrero Street, who stares at me with the kind of look my older cousin July would describe as utter disdain. But I don't care. I have to get close to the sisters. I want to ask them so many questions about Bulgaria, about the plane trip to Cuba, about their school back in Sofia. I want to ask them what they do back home, whether they go to the cinema almost every night like my friends and I do, or whether they own a television set. I want to ask what it's like to be able to travel.

When I turn up at the cinema with the rest of the neigh-bourhood kids on Saturday night, they are there—the Bulgarian sisters, the girl from General Marrero Street, who is now their full-time guide and bodyguard, and a few other girls from school who glow with exclusivity and pretend to giggle, and who are wearing their best dresses and even ribbons in their coarse, dark Cuban hair so they can impress the Bulgarian sisters. And everyone in the cinema, even the older teenagers with their girlfriends and the smattering of parents, points and whispers at *las niñas bulgaras* who pretend not to notice but how can they not?

Finally the lights go down and the shorts and the newsreel start and then the feature film. Amazingly, tonight it's a film from Eastern Europe, probably from the German Democratic Republic, where the cities are modern, covered in snow and where everyone looks well dressed and has glowing pink skin and blonde hair and lives in a stylish apartment given to them by the government because they are a good, loyal communist. I wonder, here in the dark, whether the film has been chosen especially because the Bulgarian girls are in the audience.

Later, when it's over and my friends and I walk out, I can see them standing at the front, smiling again as people wave, and listening to the girl from General Marrero Street explain something or other. I try to get close to them, perhaps to ask them about the film, or just to hang around with them, but there is no way I can because the girl from General Marrero Street is there and when she sees me, she purses her lips so they almost disappear, then she says something to the group and everyone turns around and walks up the street, so I have to remain with my group of loud, silly friends who keep making stupid noises and running along the middle of the street—they would never do that in Berlin!—and making fun of passers-by, embarrassing me like you wouldn't believe, because I am sure the Bulgarian girls, with their soft, white skin and their blonde hair, I am sure they can still see me and they are wondering to themselves, in their sophisticated Eastern European way, why these boys, these loud Cuban boys, are so immature. I hate my friends and I hate the girl from General Marrero Street.

Months later, when the Bulgarian girls have left Banes to head back home to the snow and the bare trees, when everyone at school has started to forget them, when the girl from General Marrero Street is no longer the most popular girl in class, I get my revenge, as I knew I would. As happens all the time, the teacher has chosen some students in the class to help her mark exams. I don't think this is all that fair, frankly, but apparently it's part of encouraging the best and brightest to take revolutionary responsibility at an early age, or something like that, so a couple of other students and I are chosen to help the teacher mark the exams. Each of us is given a bundle of exam papers to mark after school. I flick through the papers I have been given, all written in pencil because you can't get pens in Cuba, and that is when I notice, right there, on the right hand side at the top of the page, the name. And I smile and then I smile some more as I sharpen my red pencil, the thick red pencil we have been told we must use for marking. It's the girl from General Marrero Street. And I am about to mark her exam.

16 · THE GREAT
REVOLUTIONARY OFFENSIVE

Years later, when I am older and living outside Cuba, I realise that 1968 was what historians like to describe as a momentous year in the capitalist West—a year of student demonstrations across much of Western Europe and of upheaval in the United States as the Vietnam War escalated and so, too, the number of American casualties. There was change in the air even in Eastern Europe, with the Czech Communist Party moving towards what they called 'socialism with a human face', to the dismay of the hard old men in Moscow who promptly sent in tanks to quash what would become known as the Prague Spring. In Cuba, 1968 is also a memorable year, and not just for the García family.

On 13 March Fidel addresses students at Havana University, an address that is broadcast everywhere. You can hear his voice wherever you go in Banes, up and down the streets, booming out of television sets or from the radio. Whenever Fidel speaks, everyone else shuts up, and so far he has been speaking for hours. This time, Fidel is talking again about wanting to build a new man—*un hombre nuevo*—which still makes me think *El Maxímo*

Líder must have some ingenious socialist plan to build human robots, just like he has plans to build a giant cow and then a miniature cow, and a giant pineapple that is sweeter and juicer than capitalist pineapples, and tropical strawberries each the size of a pear. But I know that what Fidel is really talking about is me, and my brother and all my friends in the neighbourhood. He wants to educate us—the future of Cuba, he says—to become the new men of tomorrow: hardworking, uncomplaining, not interested in money or material things, and ready to fight against the imperialists anywhere in the world. Heroic men, just like Che.

The more Fidel speaks, the more animated he seems to get and the clearer his message becomes: it's obvious that he is a very, very disappointed man. No doubt shaking his head, Fidel says Cubans are far too undisciplined, too unproductive, too busy spending money on rum and beer, listening to *boleros* and *rumbas* all day. Too much time dancing in the streets. Is this any way to build socialism? We are so unproductive, he says, we are now being left behind by our communist brothers and sisters in Eastern Europe. We have been very poor and unproductive revolutionaries, he says, but that is about to change.

It doesn't take long to discover what Fidel has in mind. It's called the Great Revolutionary Offensive—*la Ofensiva Revolucionaria*.

Now, Fidel wants everyone in Cuba to work harder and to stop being interested in money and to stop spending the money they have on alcohol and music. He says if we all work harder, he will abolish money sometime in the future because money is bad. Boys with long hair are bad, too, and so is tight, provocative clothing like miniskirts, because they only encourage young Cubans to become lazy and decadent. Dancing to foreign music and reading capitalist books and magazines that find their way into Cuba are also bad because these books and magazines spread dangerous imperialist thoughts. Just because you are young doesn't mean you can go around doing nothing, either, Fidel is saying. From now on, everyone has to become true revolutionaries. What's more, if you don't agree or if you refuse to become a better revolutionary, then the police will come to your house, tell you to pack up your things and send you to cut sugarcane in the countryside until you see the error of your ways and start behaving like a socialist. It's called rectification, which sounds like very serious business to me.

Some of the things Fidel is saying don't make a lot of sense, to be honest. Like boys having long hair. Ever since we were babies, my brother and I have been getting our hair cut by Rigo, the barber who also cuts my father's hair, because he is the best barber in Banes. His hair is always combed just right and he is always talking about baseball and every now and then, when he spies a good-looking girl walking past his barber shop, Rigo will silence his dancing scissors, shake his head slowly and whistle at the girl, which is what most men do in Cuba when they want to show just how *macho* they are. My brother and I always get the same haircut from Rigo: a *malanguita*, which is the Cuban version of a very short back and sides. No decadent long hair for the García boys, that's for sure. But in the documentaries and newsreels we watch at the cinema before the main feature, there is always footage of young people marching in Paris and Washington, protesting against the imperialists, throwing rocks at police and carrying big photographs of Marx and even, believe it or not, of Che. And all those demonstrators have long hair! I can see it with my very own eyes, so what I can't understand is this: how can those young people be real revolutionaries like Che when they have long hair and wear tight jeans and miniskirts that are strictly forbidden in Cuba? I am sure that if those demonstrators lived in Cuba, they would be sent off by Fidel to cut sugarcane until they embraced the benefits of rectification.

Now Fidel is saying he is worried about bars. He says that nearly ten years after *el Triunfo*, there are still nine hundred and fifty-five bars in Havana owned by bartenders who are capitalists at heart and who just want to make money selling alcohol to people who should be cutting sugarcane instead. Bar owners don't believe in socialism, he says. This has got to stop. I have no idea how Fidel knows there are nine hundred and fifty-five bars in Havana or how he knows that all nine hundred and fifty-five bar owners are not very good revolutionaries—he says they are *lumpen*, which is a new word for me but I am sure it cannot be good. Everyone in the audience is now applauding and shouting, Fidel! Fidel! probably because they think the speech is over, but Fidel doesn't stop there. He is also worried about people who own hot food stands, known as *timbiriches* in Cuba. There is one of those stands near the Parque Cárdenas in Banes that sells hot dogs and a type of burger called *fritas* and sometimes, if you are lucky, even ice cream.

Fidel says an investigation by the Revolution has found that ninety-five point one per cent of people who own these *timbiriches* are *gusanos*. Not ninety-five per cent, but ninety-five point one per cent. They mix with anti-social elements, he says, have counter-revolutionary ideas and most—does he pause for effect?—most want to leave the country. I am amazed Fidel knows so much about hot food stands but that is the way it is with Fidel: he knows lots about everything. Is this any way to build socialism? he asks the audience, and the audience claps and yells, so Fidel asks them another question: Are we going to construct socialism or are we going to construct hot food stands? And the audience yells out: Socialism! Socialism! Socialism! And that's when Fidel decides, right there and then, that all bars and all *timbiriches* and all private shops will be closed down. It's at that moment that Fidel decides that the Revolution will eliminate all private trade. I wonder what the other four point nine per cent of hot food stand owners are thinking . . .

I have no idea what Fidel's announcement will mean for my parents and their shop. I know they are not very good revolutionaries at home, and I know they have probably thought about leaving Cuba, and I know they sometimes say capitalist things, but it's not as if they are out in the street looking for trouble or attacking the Revolution. They may be *gusanos* at heart but they are not *lumpen*, I am sure, and they are certainly not *elementos antisociales*—anti-social elements—which is the way the newspaper and everyone else is now referring to people who spend too much time pretending they are capitalists, listening to foreign music, and wearing colourful shirts or very short skirts.

On the radio over the next few days, all the talk is about this Great Revolutionary Offensive, and how we must all be vigilant against people who may be a danger to the Revolution, even here in Banes where everyone knows everyone else. We have been told to keep our eyes open for trouble-makers, like *chicos melenudos*—boys with long hair who play guitar and sing foreign pop songs—and *jipis*, who dance to what they say on radio is 'epileptic music'. If we see any, we must report them at once to the Committee for the Defence of the Revolution.

I heard from one of my best friends at school and no, I can't tell you his name because he will get into trouble with his mother, that the *milicianos* in Havana have been arresting anyone who behaves or looks suspiciously like an *elemento antisocial* and sending them off to cut sugarcane so they can become better revolutionaries. My friend, who seems to know everything that's going on, says his mother told him that her cousin who lives in Havana told her that police had conducted major raids, or *redadas*, on famous people, including well-known writers whose names mean nothing to me, and singers. Even some television presenters, believe it or not, were taken away because they were too *efeminado*, which is the polite term Cubans use when they don't want to say *maricones*, which is what everyone else calls homosexuals. If you are an *efeminado*, my friend says, then watch out because sooner or later they will find you, cut your long hair and take away all your hippie music and force you to walk like a real man.

In all of Banes I only know one *efeminado*, which is as it should be since I am sure Cuban men are all real men—just like Fidel—and we like to talk about baseball and drink rum and play dominos with our mates and make love, Cuban love, but only to women, you understand? The *efeminado* I know is the cousin of one of my neighbourhood friends and although he is older than we are—he must be at least sixteen—every time he visits he plays with us, and after a while we all sit down on the steps outside the pastry shop next door to our house in Flor Crombet Street and talk about movies and books and music and anything else that comes into his head because he is the one who always does the talking. I can tell he is an anti-social element because I can see the way he rolls his eyes skywards when he doesn't believe you, or the way he laughs out loud so that everyone in the street can hear him. And the way he walks! My God, it's like he is dancing or something, which is not—I repeat, not—the way men are supposed to walk in Banes, or anywhere else in Cuba!

Sometimes, when we get bored or when we think he is being too *efeminado*, we call him names like *maricón* and *mariquita* and tell him, just jokingly, that we will report him to the Committee for the Defence of the Revolution, but in reality he doesn't care much. I know there are some mothers in the neighbourhood who don't like my friend's cousin hanging around our group of younger boys when he visits because they say he is a bad influence, whatever that means. The mother of one of my friends is always rushing up to wherever we are and taking her son away from the group, pulling him away, and asking him, Did he touch you?, pointing to the only *efeminado* we know in Banes. Tell me, *niño*, did that *mariquita* touch you anywhere? And don't you dare lie to me or else . . . We don't understand what all the fuss is about.

My friend's cousin stopped coming around during that year when all of Cuba went crazy, the year of the Great Revolutionary Offensive. I don't know if someone reported him to the Committee for the Defence of the Revolution for being a *lumpen* and they sent him away. Perhaps he stopped being an *efeminado* and became a good revolutionary and stopped rolling his eyes and walking funny and not caring what anyone said about him. I can't tell you. I never saw him again.

★

When I get back from school today, my father is home instead of being at work in the shop, and I can tell from the moment I walk in through the door that he is not in a good mood. He is talking to himself, saying things like, *¿Quien lo hiba a pensar?*—Who would have thought it? He tells us that when he turned up at the shop this morning there were two *milicianos* at the front, one on each side of the door, carrying guns, which all *milicianos* do, and looking determined. When my father said, Good morning, what's going on here?, they called him *compañero*, which my father thinks is always a bad sign, and then they told him that on the orders of the Revolutionary Government they were taking over his shop. Not just his shop, really. Every privately owned shop in the street and in the street just behind it and every shop across Banes and the whole of Cuba—the Revolution is taking over fifty-five thousand small shops and bars and cafes that are still owned and run by their capitalist owners because this is all part of the Great Revolutionary Offensive.

Now Fidel's speech makes a lot more sense to me. Not to my father. He can't believe it. He says when the *milicianos* said, Hand over your keys, he could tell they were not joking, not even smiling, so he handed over the keys and asked them, What now?, and they looked at him and said, *Compañero*, go home. Go home and wait for further instructions. Go home and wait, while we build a New Man.

If my father is incredulous, my mother is totally beaten. Humiliated. She has her own story to tell: when she turned up at the shop to see what was going on, because she could not believe what my father had just told her, the *milicianos* were still there but she was met by a woman called Albita, who used to work in the shop some years ago, when there was stuff on the shelves for sale. Albita, who was wearing her olive green *miliciana* uniform, was standing by the door looking quite satisfied with herself. When my mother tried to enter the shop Albita stood in front of her, placed her hands on her ample hips and said, *Compañera*, this shop now belongs to the People and you—here she pointed at my mother—you will no longer be allowed to exploit your workers. *¡Se acabó la explotación!* Which would have been more than enough for my mother to burst into tears of frustration and anger but she didn't because she was not going to give Albita the satisfaction of seeing her cry. So she turned around and went back home, too. To wait for instructions from Albita.

Can you believe it? she asks my father. Can you believe that anyone would say *that* to me? Can you believe that anyone would accuse *me*, who has worked so hard to build that shop up, of exploiting my employees? She sounds angry but you

141

can tell she has given up. You can tell she thinks it's all too, too hard.

There is no consolation in knowing that she is not the only shopkeeper to lose her shop. All the other small shops in Banes now belong to the People too. Like *Bar Feria*, where my father celebrated the birth of his first-born, and the paper shop *La Marquesita* where they sell books about Fidel, and the *Isla de Cuba* hardware store and the pastry shop next door and, of course, the hot food stand near the park. That is gone too. Even the small *guarapería* is gone, the one up the road that is always noisy and dark and full of people waiting their turn to taste the sweet and sticky sugarcane juice that one of my uncles says is the true taste of Cuba. No more capitalism.

As far as my father is concerned, this is the last straw. He has had enough. For nearly ten years, he says, sounding more incredulous than upset, he has been hanging on, hoping that things would change. But he knows there will be no change. Not in a hurry. He is determined that we leave Cuba—which is easier said than done. My uncle Rodolfo and my aunt Mirta, who now live in New York, have been encouraging my parents to make the decision for months. We have saved up the money, they say, we will lend you what you need for the airfares. Start the paperwork!

All that time, my mother has resisted. She doesn't want to leave Cuba because she doesn't want to leave her brothers and her other sisters behind, probably forever. She knows what happens when you apply to leave Cuba: we will officially become *gusanos* and my father will be sent away almost immediately to a labour camp somewhere far from Banes to cut sugarcane for the Revolution for at least two or three years, or until someone in Havana says to Fidel, *Comandante en Jefe*, you can let these people go now; they have paid their dues.

She knows she will be left alone at home with two children who can be quite a handful at the best of times. She knows it will become even more difficult to find food on her own. She knows she will miss my father. But now, the decision has been made for her, although it is a decision no one will know about for some time yet. She is still reluctant but she is giving in, bit by bit—taking the shop away from her, the shop she worked so hard to build up, and then, she says in disbelief, to be humiliated as she has been in her own shop, in her own town, ¡*Dios mio!* This could well be the end of the revolutionary road for my normally non-political mother.

I know what my parents are talking about and I know they will argue about it in the months ahead because my mother will change her mind and then change it again, but I keep quiet because neither of them has even thought of asking me, let alone my brother, whether we want to leave Cuba. I am glad they don't ask because if they did, I would say no, I would tell them that I don't want to go to no stinking capitalist country, thank you, because I am happy where I am. I like my school and my house and my friends and I don't want to leave. I don't want other kids in school calling me a *gusano*. I want to be like everyone else. I don't want to be different.

⭐

My father no longer owns or works in what used to be his and my mother's shop but the Revolution has found him a new job: he has been made foreman at the biscuit and noodle factory in Banes. He thinks it's funny because while he is a very good shopkeeper, he has absolutely no experience in running a biscuit and noodle factory. But that's the way decisions are made in Cuba, he says: they take you out of a job you can do and put you in a job you have no idea about. And then Fidel complains about low productivity! No wonder it's taking so long to build the New Man.

My brother and I are mighty pleased with the new job, though. It means that every day my father arrives home with a big brown paper bag full of biscuits. No queues and no *libreta*. My father is not alone in this. He tells my mother that half the biscuits and noodles that are produced at the factory every day simply disappear, which means the people working there must be taking a lot of biscuits and noodles home to their families. Cubans don't call it stealing. They call it *resolviendo*; I don't think there is a suitably direct English term for it, but it means something like 'making do'. And if you have ever had to queue for two or three hours in the sun, with no hat or umbrella to protect you, so you can buy whatever is on offer that day, then you'd understand exactly what *resolviendo* means too. That's what my father says.

Meanwhile, my mother has been ordered to return to the shop she used to own, where she must report for revolutionary duty carrying on as if nothing had happened. It's not something my very fatalistic mother is happy about, especially when she gets there and finds that Albita is now the new boss, *la Administradora*. This is what has happened to every one of the shops taken over during the Great Revolutionary Offensive: the owners now report to someone like Albita, who is wearing her *miliciana* outfit just to prove she really is the Boss and gets to tell my mother what to do.

There is just one small consolation as far as my mother is concerned. Within weeks the shop will close. There is nothing to sell so there are no customers coming in through the door, not even the old *guajiros* from the nearby farms who used to buy so much on credit, and even in socialist Cuba, even in the middle of the Great Revolutionary Offensive, it's not a good thing to have an empty shop with nothing to sell. So one morning when my mother arrives to report for her revolutionary duty, she is told the shop is now closed. They put a big lock on the door and post a *miliciano* at the front to make sure no one breaks in and steals the light fittings and the glass cabinets and the timber shelving. And just like that, *Retacería García* ceases to be.

★

Richard Nixon has been elected President of the United States, which means that he is automatically an enemy of the Revolution, like all other presidents of the United States. His name is everywhere, on radio and in the *Granma* newspaper where they have replaced the X in Nixon with a funny sign that I soon discover is a swastika. I don't get the connection at first but my uncle Rogelio, who knows a lot about history, explains, in his usual patient way, that Nixon is a fascist, which is the worst thing you can imagine, almost as bad, I am sure, as being called a *maricón*. Or *lumpen*.

According to *Granma*, which is the only daily newspaper in Cuba, Nixon wants to crush the Revolution and return Cuba to the days when it was an American colony. Nothing good can come from *El Norte*, if you believe *Granma*—the poor are always being exploited or starving to death. Not that we buy *Granma*, which describes itself under the big, red title as the Official Organ of the Communist Party. My father refuses to buy it because, he says, while it costs only a couple of cents, it's all rubbish. Propaganda! It means I only read the paper if I go to the library or when I visit my aunt Adelina, who buys the paper every day as you would do if you were a good revolutionary.

Much as I enjoy reading, I suspect my father may be right:

there are not a lot of pictures in *Granma*, no comics and no news about what Los Zafiros are up to, even though they are the most popular musical group in Cuba today and famous all over Eastern Europe. Instead, there are reports about how an electricity plant in the city of Cienfuegos has met its production target; about heroic Vietnamese peasants—they are always heroic in *Granma*—killing a truckload of Yankee soldiers with a few bamboo sticks; and about how thousands of poor people sleep on the streets of Washington while the rich spend millions of dollars on dog food. That's on a normal day. Every few days Fidel gives one of his four- or five-hour speeches and the following morning *Granma* publishes the entire transcript, which fills up most of the paper.

Sometimes my parents relent and buy a copy or two of *Granma*, but only when we run out of toilet paper. My father cuts the pages up into squares and sticks them on a nail by the toilet bowl. I am sure this is not very revolutionary but even my uncle Rogelio does it, so I assume it is okay. Still, those clever journalists at *Granma* have the last laugh—they print the newspaper on really thin paper and the headlines are always in big, revolutionary red.

We don't have a television set at home and my brother and I think this is the worst thing ever. In truth, the worst thing would be to have an American television set like the one at the house of one of my mother's aunts but have no spare parts to replace broken tubes, so that the box sits there in the living room but you can't watch anything. We get to see television at my friend's house where they have a new set made somewhere in East Germany. It looks big and clunky and even older than my mother's aunt's old American set that doesn't work any more.

My friend's mother got her television set because she is a

good revolutionary. That is the only way to get a television set in Cuba, or a new radio or lounge chairs, or the most prized possession of all: a new Polish refrigerator. You can't buy these things—the Revolution gives them to you, thanks to Fidel, but only if you deserve them. If you become the most productive worker in the factory, or if you cut the most sugarcane in the district, or if you are the busiest nurse in the local hospital, then someone in the Communist Party nominates you as an exceptional worker and eventually you get your East German television set to take home, or even a holiday at Varadero beach. If you are really, really good, you become a National Hero of Labour, get to shake hands with Fidel on television and win a trip to Russia. But you have to be as good as bricklayer Rafael Cuevas, who became National Hero of Labour because he could lay 2190 bricks in just four hours. That's a lot of bricks.

Of course, apart from working harder you also need to be a good revolutionary—you need a good *expediente laboral* to confirm that, yes, you have been to meetings at work to discuss Marx or to meetings outside the Party House to denounce evil Richard Nixon. Which means that we will never get a television set because although my father works hard producing biscuits and noodles for the people of Banes, I am sure he will never become a Hero of Labour: let's face it, he has never been to one of those meetings to discuss Marx.

I know my father gets all the news he needs at night, after dinner, when he turns on the radio very, very low and fiddles with the knobs until, as if by magic, he gets the Voice of America, which I am shocked to discover later is an American station! Even I know it's illegal to listen to American radio stations so I can't understand why my father insists on it when he knows he can get into trouble if anyone catches him.

My mother, who worries about everything, is always

telling my father to turn the volume down some more because otherwise the neighbours will hear. You can tell she is scared because if someone knocks on the front door she runs to the radio to either turn it off or move the dial up or down until we get back to Radio Progreso, the Cuban station. It must be worth the trouble because my father says listening to the Voice of America is the only way to know what is really happening in Cuba.

Whenever my brother and I ask why we don't have a television set, my parents tells us that there is nothing to watch on television. Only speeches by Fidel, and we can hear those on radio or read them in *Granma*, page after page. We say, yes, but they also show *muñequitos*—cartoons—and serials and comedies like *Detrás de la Fachada*, which is the most popular program on television, and they tell us, Don't worry about it. But we do. I think my parents' brains have been taken over by Nixon and his X that turns into a swastika, and by the Voice of America.

It's amazing how those Americans twist the truth—and how easily they have hypnotised my father! Despite my mother's protests, he has been listening to the Voice of America again, which says that Russian tanks have invaded Czechoslovakia and that the Czech people want to withdraw from the Warsaw Pact, which every school child in Cuba knows is the pact that protects the Soviet Union and the other fraternal countries of Eastern Europe from Richard Nixon. Of course, I don't believe anything they say on the Voice of America. I know they are twisting the truth because their story is very different to the story we get to hear on Cuban radio, where Fidel explains what really happened. He says Czechoslovakia was being taken over by liberals and imperialists who are, as you know, the enemies of socialism. That is why the real communists in Prague asked the Soviet Union to come in with their tanks and help them protect socialism from the Americans. Fidel says the Cuban Revolution and the entire Cuban people—*el Pueblo entero*—is right behind the Soviet Union. Obviously, no one has bothered to ask my father.

17 · A *MILICIANO* AT THE DOOR

A *miliciano* is at the door, which is never a good thing in Cuba. Both my parents know immediately what the visit is all about—the police are now aware we have decided to leave Cuba. They know this because, as with everything else in Cuba, the police always know what you are up to. Sometimes even before you do.

The first step once you decide to leave—the essential first step—is to get a relative or a friend overseas who is willing to deposit money into your account in Cuba because you will need that money to secure plane tickets. You can't even start the paperwork officially unless you have the money for the airfares, and the tickets must be paid for with capitalist dollars rather than revolutionary Cuban *pesos*. So my aunt Mirta and my uncle Rodolfo went to their bank in New York and deposited over US$3000—a fortune, says my father—into our family's bank account in Cuba. As soon as that happened, the bank told the police, which they are obliged to do, and that is why there is a *miliciano* standing at our front door asking my father, *Compañero*, are you really leaving Cuba?

Making the decision to leave Cuba has not been an easy one for my parents, especially for my mother, who is torn, as my father knew she would be, between wanting to get her sons out of Cuba and not wanting to leave behind the rest of her family. She also knows that applying to leave Cuba could compromise her brothers, especially my uncle Papi, who is moving fast up the Communist Party ladder in our province. So, she has been avoiding the inevitable, keeping quiet the news of our decision to leave, which has been quite a feat since my father has had to start organising the endless round of paperwork, and we have all had to have our photographs taken for our passports. But there is no hiding any more. Now, the police are here and my father is confirming that, yes, we have applied to leave Cuba. My uncles and aunts will find out soon enough and so, too, will my teachers, my friends at school, the neighbours, the Committee for the Defence of the Revolution, and the rest of Banes. We are now officially *gusanos*.

The *miliciano* at the door is polite but firm. He tells my parents that he and one of his colleagues will come back later to *pasar balance*: to take stock of everything we own, from the plates and glasses in the kitchen cabinets to the pillows in the bedrooms. Even our clothes—how many shirts? How many pairs of shoes? And, of course, the big appliances, like our old fridge and the big, crackly radio on which my father listens to the Voice of America. Every single item is going to be noted down, a meticulous process that will take hours. So, the *miliciano* says, don't even think about taking anything out of the house until we get back. Nothing. As if we would . . .

Then the policeman turns to my father and tells him that he should pack up his working clothes, his toothbrush, too, some food and work boots and present himself tomorrow morning, on the dot of four, when it is still dark, down at the Parque Cárdenas.

As happens with anyone who applies to leave, what this means is that my father has now lost his job at the noodle and biscuit factory. No more biscuits! From now on he will have to work in the countryside, along with hundreds of other *gusanos*, until Fidel decides my father has paid his debt to the Revolution and is free to depart.

I knew this moment was coming, of course. It's what happened to my friend Jorgito's father. One day he was at home, sitting on his veranda in one of those old-fashioned rocking chairs that Cubans like so much, and the next he was gone. Off to an *albergue*—a labour camp—somewhere in Oriente province. I knew this would happen to my father too, but still the news comes as a huge shock to all of us, especially my mother, whose face is now contorted in anguish as she tries, without success, to hold back her tears.

Later in the day, the police come knocking again, as promised, to take stock of our belongings, except they are accompanied by *La Compañera* from the Committee for the Defence of the Revolution, who can barely hide her excitement. I imagine she is thinking to herself, I was right, I was right, the Garcías were *gusanos* after all. As they move from room to room, making sure they don't miss anything that belongs to the People, I can see both my parents getting increasingly anxious. I know my father feels humiliated too, which is probably what this process is intended to achieve. To me it seems absurd—who would want my old shoes?—but neither my parents nor I nor my brother say anything. And so the *balance* goes on and on, until every piece of furniture, every utensil and every item in the bathroom is categorised and noted down on the official forms.

What the very efficient policemen don't know, of course, is that my mother has already spirited away some of the few real valuables she still owns, those she hasn't yet exchanged for food, like some of her old jewellery, which she has given to one of my aunts for safekeeping. Not that my mother intends to take anything out of Cuba. One thing is made absolutely clear to us: when the time comes to leave Cuba, we can take with us only one suitcase per person. No money, no jewellery, no valuables of any type. All that belongs to the Revolution now, and if we are caught taking valuables out then, well, we are in big trouble because they can turn us around right there at the airport, snatch our airplane tickets from our very hands and send us back to Banes. Despite this, we keep hearing stories of women who have carefully hidden diamonds in the lining of their dresses or inside their beehive hairstyles; or men who have had their dentists drill their good teeth so that the holes can then be filled with pure gold. I don't know if the stories are true or not but I am sure my parents are too cautious—and too poor—to do anything so silly.

Now, when the police finally leave and my father starts to pack up his *mochila*, his backpack, it hits me that we won't see him again for quite a while, that this is the new life we have to get accustomed to, at least for the next year if not longer. Much longer. And I wonder how my father is going to cope in the countryside. He was born in the countryside and he is used to hard work, but it's still a long way from supervising other people making noodles and biscuits to having to get up at five every morning to go out and cut sugarcane under the hot Cuban sun all day long—and for no pay.

And how are we going to cope? We have no idea where he is going or for how long, and we won't find out until he gets there and somehow manages to ring one of our neighbours and ask them to tell us where he is. And when he gets to wherever he is taken, he will not be allowed to leave. He can write to us and we can go and visit him on some weekends, depending on how far he is taken, but he is not allowed to leave the labour camp, except once every forty-five days when he gets a five-day pass.

How will my mother and my brother and I cope without him at home? I know my mother is strong but I am still worried that without my father we won't have enough money to buy food when it's our turn at the *bodega*. I worry that we will starve to death. I worry that there won't be anyone at home big enough and strong enough to protect my mother and my brother and me. I feel like crying but I don't because I can still remember very clearly what my uncle Rogelio said to me last night when we visited to tell him and my aunt Adelina the news. He looked at me and said, using his serious tone of voice, Now your father is going away, you will have to look after your mother and your brother . . . You are the man of the house now. And I stood there, looking at him and wanting to cry right there and then because, let me tell you, they were the scariest words I had ever heard.

★

My aunt Nidia has decided she wants to leave Cuba too. She says she can't stand it any more and she wants to get out as soon as possible. This is not good news for my father. In fact, he thinks it is a disaster as my aunt Nidia will apply to leave Cuba with us, as part of our family group—*nucleo familiar*—and he is not happy. Not that he can do much about it, as my aunt Mirta and uncle Rodolfo in New York have already sent the money for the plane tickets for all five of us.

My father and my aunt don't get along. In truth, my aunt doesn't seem to get along with too many members of her extended family, which may explain why my mother and my other aunts often refer to her as *la oveja negra de la familia*—the black sheep of the family. She is in her late forties, and she was married once, a long time ago, but my mother says that did not last very long and ended in divorce, as everyone in the family kind of expected, apparently. Now, she lives in the old family house on Presidente Zayas Avenue, with my uncle Rogelio and my aunt Adelina and my cousin July but in truth she seems to spend a lot of time dressed up as if she is going to a party, visiting her many friends around Banes and gossiping about other people in the town.

She seems to know not just our family's secrets but other people's secrets too, and she passes them on, like the way she points at a woman who lives on her own in a house a few doors down from us, just near the park, and says, You know, she is *la querida* of so and so, using the Cuban term for mistress, and he is married and he won't leave his wife, and now he and his family want to leave Cuba, which is just the sort of secret my mother thinks my aunt should not be telling a boy of my tender years. I think my aunt Nidia is a *solterona*—an old maid—but I never call her this to her face because I know she won't like it. Besides, she has had many marriage proposals at different times, very good marriage proposals from very suitable young men around Banes, or at least that's what she tells me and anyone else who cares to listen. I have learnt that it's best not to contradict my aunt.

I think my aunt is great fun because she is unpredictable, doing things you would never expect her to do, like taking me out for ice cream but refusing to queue, instead walking right up to the counter and demanding to be served immediately because, *por favor, señor*, can't you see that this boy here is too small to be waiting for hours just so he can get an ice cream? Somehow, my aunt Nidia always gets away with it and then as we walk away from the ice cream place, she looks down at me and winks, and then takes out of her bag a pressed, white linen handkerchief that smells of expensive eau de cologne from *antes del Triunfo*, and wipes my chin clean.

My aunt sometimes scares me, too, because I have seen her get very angry and start shouting and threatening, and it's not something you expect either, so when it happens I make sure I get out of the way. She used to fight with my uncle Rodolfo all the time but since he is now in the United States, she fights with my father, over even the smallest, silliest things, and she always ends the fight with a comment about how my mother made such a mistake, a *huge* mistake, she adds for emphasis, marrying him, which of course only makes my father angrier. Then my aunt turns on her heels and walks away as if the whole thing was finished and she had been declared the winner, which I guess in a way she was, leaving my father behind about to explode in frustration and saying things like, *¡Esa mujer! Le falta un tornillo*— that woman has a screw loose.

So I can understand why my father isn't happy that my aunt Nidia is now part of our *nucleo familiar* because he knows, like my mother knows, although she won't say so, that this will mean trouble: since we are all linked as a family group in the paperwork, it's going to be almost impossible to pretend my aunt is not part of the family. What scares my father is that my aunt is not the type you would call discreet, which is what you must be when you officially become a *gusano*—you shut up because everything you say will be reported back to someone and that someone has the power to take away your passport or your permission papers, and keep you in Cuba. But this doesn't worry my aunt one bit. She still spends her time visiting her friends and gossiping, criticising the Revolution and even Fidel, which sends my mother into a state of panic because you just never know who might be listening. Are you crazy? my mother says to my aunt. How can you say those things? And in public! Don't you know that saying those things might mean we don't get permission to leave? Then my aunt turns on her heels and walks away as usual.

I know it won't take long before my father and my aunt clash again—and it's not something I look forward to since I can already tell that my totally unpredictable aunt Nidia is destined to do something silly or say something silly that will result in Fidel refusing to let us leave Cuba.

18 · WITH FIDEL IN THE SUGARCANE FIELDS

We now know where my father has been sent. He is at a labour camp in an area called La Gabina, which is near the town of Bayamo. It's so far from Banes and transport is so bad that he could just as easily be in Russia, according to my mother, who is not coping well with the fact that her husband has been taken away from her. My brother and I also miss him, and we keep asking my mother whether she has any idea when he is coming back home. Tomorrow night? Next week? She doesn't know but she says that as soon as we can, we will go and visit him and take him some extra clothes and some food because she has heard the food in the camps is *malísima*. Very bad.

We also know there are about one hundred and fifty other *gusanos* with my father at La Gabina, and a handful of *milicianos* whose job is to make sure the *gusanos* work hard, stay out of trouble and pay their dues to the Revolution. This means getting up at the crack of dawn every morning, having a breakfast of black coffee and a chunk of bread, and then going out into the nearby cane fields to cut sugarcane until six in the evening, when they return to the camp for dinner, a shower if there is any water left, and bed. Next day it starts all over again.

Not having our father at home is tough. I hate it, especially when most of my friends in the neighbourhood have their fathers at home. To make things worse, everyone knows that our father is not at home because he is one of those ungrateful Cubans who wants to leave for *El Norte* to eat lots of American ham and cheese in exchange for becoming a slave of capitalism, which according to the man on the radio is what happens to everyone who leaves Cuba for the United States.

While I can see that my mother misses my father, I can also see that she is trying to be strong and pretend that life goes on as normal, so she wakes us up in the morning, prepares some breakfast for us and sends us off to school, just like she always did. But she gets scared at night, which is why she has asked her best friend, Hilda, to come and stay with us. My brother and I think it's great because we love Hilda—unlike my mother, she doesn't make too much fuss if we don't finish all our dinner. With my mother, on the other hand, well, you must eat all of your food because she thinks my brother and I are too skinny and, let me tell you, no sons of hers are ever going to look as if they are so poor they don't have enough food at home. Eat! Eat!

I don't think we are all that skinny but there is not much point arguing with a Cuban mother when it comes to food. Even with rationing, my mother somehow always manages to find enough food to feed her boys—the occasional steak, which she fries in a little pork fat with onions, or chicken legs which she cooks with rice and some yellow colouring to make *arroz con pollo.*

Because we now know where my father is and because we now know that he won't be coming home for quite a while, my mother is making plans for her, Hilda, my brother and me to go and visit him on Sunday, the only day that he is allowed a visit from his family. It's going to be difficult getting to La Gabina because it's a long way away and no bus service takes you there. Don't ask me how, but my mother has found a way of getting us on a truck that leaves Banes at four in the morning and will take us to a town close to where the labour camp is. From there we will have to hitch a ride in another truck or a cart or whatever comes along until we get to the camp.

I am looking forward to seeing my father again but I am not convinced we can make it, and I keep imagining the four of us getting lost in the middle of some huge sugarcane field far from home, never to be found again until it's too late: all that's left will be the skeletons of two kids and two women carrying a *jaba* full of decomposed food. I don't mention any of this to my mother, of course, because she will probably get upset and tell me to stop being silly and stop scaring my brother with stories about death. In any case, I figure she has plenty to worry about already.

When we finally arrive at La Gabina, I think we are in the wrong place. In my mind I had visions of a concentration camp like the ones I have seen on old Russian films about the Second World War, with electric fences, high towers and guards in black uniforms holding on tight to menacing, hungry dogs. Instead, it's a pretty open camp, although there are still *milicianos* around and they *are* carrying guns. But this is Cuba, the sun is shining and warm, the sky is sparkling blue, like Cuban skies are supposed to be, so we just walk through the entrance as though we are going on a picnic, along with fifty or sixty other families who have also made the trek from God knows where all carrying containers heavy with home-made food and *jabas* with extra clothes.

My brother and I quickly spot our father among the large group standing just inside the gates. We rush to him and give him a hug and kiss his face, which is now rough, sunburnt and spiky, and tell him we miss him a lot. It's good to see him, and we think my mother is going to be happy too, but instead she bursts into tears at the sight of just how skinny my father is. Where has her husband gone? He is turning into a skeleton, she says, and cries some more.

We spend the day with my father, who introduces us to other *gusanos* who have now become his friends before taking us on a tour of the camp. Not that there is much to see. In the middle, there is a huge open-air building with a thatched roof and dirt floor and what seems like hundreds of simple bunk beds with canvas mattresses. Underneath the beds, or next to them, there are wooden boxes or big bags in which the men keep all their belongings. They don't have much because no one at the camp, not even the guards, knows how long they will be at La Gabina, or where they are likely to go next. It's like a travelling troupe of gypsies, moving from cane field to cane field, says Hilda, except these aren't gypsies and the further they go, the more difficult it will be for us to travel to see my father.

As my mother unpacks the food she has brought and starts to pack up dirty clothes to take home to wash, my father is telling us that the work is hard but you adjust to it, although I think he is just saying that so we can all feel better. But the food, he says, the food is bad. *Malísima*. For the first couple of weeks all they got was a very liquid stew made from peas known as *chicharos*. The stew had no meat in it, apart for the floating larvae, my father says, which is enough for my brother and me to start giggling because we think he is joking, but he says, No, no, it's true, they floated in the stew. He couldn't eat his stew and instead ate whatever he had left from home, which wasn't much. Eventually, he says, you either eat the *chicharos* with or without floating debris, or you go hungry. It explains why he has lost so much weight—fifteen kilos, my father says.

Over the next twenty-four months or so, my father is moved even further away, to larger labour camps where there are lots more *gusanos*, more guards, tougher work and the same awful food. The only thing that doesn't seem to change, my father says with a wry smile, is the number of latrines. There are never enough. First, he is moved to a labour camp in an area known as Casimiro, which isn't too far from La Gabina but almost impossible for us to reach; and eventually to a camp called La Brasa, where the number of *gusanos* swelled to nearly five hundred and where conditions were so primitive, especially when it rained, that my father still recoils in horror when he talks about it.

Our visit to La Gabina on this sunny Sunday is my first and only visit to my father in the countryside. My mother will visit again later but she will decide, wisely, that it's just too long and unpredictable a trip for her two boys, so we stay home, counting the days until my father gets his five-day pass and appears at the front door as if by magic, looking thin and tired but happy to be home again, at least for a couple of days. ¿*Hasta cuando*? my mother asks herself. How much longer? By the time we find our way home this Sunday, after hitching a ride on the back of a truck from La Gabina and then queuing up for what seems like an eternity to get on a bus that can take us near Banes, and then walking the last few kilometres to town, my brother and I are utterly exhausted. All I want to do is go to sleep, in my own bed.

★

I wake up in the middle of the night, startled. Someone is in the kitchen, I am sure. I am scared but I still get up and walk quietly past my mother, who is sleeping on the big bed, past the small dining area . . . As I get closer, I am sure I can hear my father in the kitchen making a cup of strong, sweet Cuban coffee like he always does, and humming that old Mexican *ranchera* he always used to sing to my brother and me when we were little to get us to go to sleep. It's the one about the cowboy who travels all over Mexico, heartbroken now that his true love has died, picking fights so he gets killed and is put out of his misery. But when I get to the kitchen, it's dark and empty and there is no one there. Perhaps it was just a dream. So I go back to my bed, wanting to cry because I miss my father but not crying because I remember what my uncle Rogelio said: I am now the man of the house.

★

I am beginning to think my parents are totally mad. Here they are, announcing they want to leave for *El Norte* when they must know that the United States is a crazy country where a small number of people are very rich and they spend all their time working with Richard Nixon, whose name has a swastika, thinking up ways of exploiting poor people around the world, even in their own country. I know all this because this is what I get taught at school, and this is what they say on radio and on television all the time.

You'd have to be crazy to want to leave Cuba, where we have the best health care system in the world, where all children go to school, which is free, and where the Revolution has done so much for the People, like providing new houses to *guajiros* in the Sierra Maestra, and teaching them how to read and write. I am sure this is why the Americans are now coming to live here. Lots of them. On television and on the newsreels we see at the Teatro Hernández they have pictures of Americans, mostly black people with big, big haircuts that would most certainly be illegal in Cuba, being welcomed to Havana airport after diverting a plane that was supposed to be flying from Newark to Miami but instead ended up being hijacked to Havana. It happens now almost every week. But in the newsreels they never say hijacking, because these brave Americans are only trying to do what I am sure most Americans would love to do: leave their corrupt, crime-ridden capitalist country where the poor go hungry and have to sleep on the streets, and come to live in Cuba, where we may be poor but value our independence and our dignity. That's what they say on television. And here are my parents trying to leave Cuba. Have they gone mad?

We look so strange, so foreign, my brother and I this Sunday. We are in the Parque Cárdenas, standing under the hot, tropical sun, squinting and uncomfortable, having our picture taken by a friend of the family who used to have his own photographic studio *antes del Triunfo*. I am wearing a navy blue blazer that is making me hot and sweaty, as I knew it would, white pants, a white shirt and—can you believe this—a bowtie. Same for my brother, except his coat is lighter and he is even more fidgety than I am.

I don't know where my mother found these outfits but here we are, the two of us, about to take First Communion; and while there is a part of me that is excited about the whole thing, I also think that standing here in the park looking like this is the most embarrassing thing imaginable on a Sunday morning in Banes. And now the picture-taking is over, we will have to walk through the centre of town—dressed like this!—to get to the church.

It's not a huge group of children taking First Communion and I am sure we are all *gusanos* because only *gusanos* go to church on Sundays. For weeks we have been learning about Christ and about drinking His blood and eating His flesh, which makes my brother giggle because he doesn't think he is ready to start drinking anyone's blood, let alone eating their flesh. Apart from my brother and me, the only other boy from our neighbourhood who is also taking First Communion today is our friend Pepitin. There are a few girls, too, looking as if they are going to get married in their lacy white dresses, and they look even more like *gusanos* than we boys do because they are also wearing gloves. Gloves! In Banes!

The church is only half full, which is about average, and most of the people sitting towards the front are old, or at least they seem old to me, which is not surprising since young people are not encouraged to come to church. As everyone knows, being a Catholic is not such a good idea in socialist Cuba. If you are a Catholic who goes to mass you can't become a member of the Union of Communist Youth, which means you will never get to be a true revolutionary and be chosen to join the Communist Party. It could be worse, of course. You could be a Jehovah's Witness and then you'd be in jail for refusing to do military service.

My mother is here in church, which is rare, but my father is not because he is still cutting sugarcane for Fidel and, anyway, he really doesn't have much time for church. *Yo creo a mi manera*, he always says to my mother—I believe in my own way—which is probably just his excuse not to have to go to church on Sundays. I can't blame him because, really, much as I like Father Emerio, who was a *barbudo* in the Sierra Maestra with Fidel, and much as I enjoy the quietness of the place, we should be cutting sugarcane like all good revolutionaries. Or at the cinema.

Instead, we are walking down the long aisle towards the altar ready to receive Christ and the Holy Spirit and listening to Father Emerio talk about God and the responsibilities we now carry as Catholics, before he calls each one of us to come closer to him and then says in a strong voice, The body of Christ, my son, and then he gently places the host—*la hostia*—on my tongue before offering the big, shiny golden cup half filled with sweet red wine which is, he says, the blood of Christ. I drink from the cup and stand there expecting something to happen, waiting to see if what I have been told is true—that Christ comes into your body and blesses you and makes you an even better Catholic—but nothing happens, except that my brother, who is behind me, gives me a push to make me move along and back to the pew where we have all been sitting waiting to become better Catholics.

I kneel, as we have been told to do, and pray to God, careful not to chew on the host because I have been told by one of the older boys that chewing your host is as mortal a sin as they come. I have been worrying for days about what to pray for. I know I don't want to sound selfish, not this first time after Communion, but I figure that God will understand that I have plenty to pray for, you know. So I pray without any shame for my father not to have to spend too much more time in the labour camp, and I pray that my mother continues to look after my brother and me the way she always does, especially with my father away, and I pray that Fidel, who I know thinks religion is the opium of the masses, will bend a little bit, just a little bit, and give us permission to leave Cuba soon . . . But not too soon because I am going to miss my friends and my family.

After mass we go out into the bright sunshine and walk a few steps to the hall next door for breakfast. It's a big breakfast, too, with *café con leche* made with real cow's milk that tastes creamy and warm and fresh and nothing, I tell you, like the powdered stuff that is all you can get with the ration book. And there is also a big *pan de madeira*, which is called a pound cake in English and which is moist and sweet; even I can tell it has been made with real eggs. It's not the type of breakfast we get at home and I have no idea how that old *barbudo* Father Emerio or the women who still wear Spanish *mantillas* to mass and who help him cook and keep the church have managed to get real eggs and real butter and real flour to make the cake, but it doesn't matter because it tastes terrific. It's like a cake made by God, which in a way it probably is, says my mother, since only God would be able to find real butter and real flour and real eggs in Banes nowadays.

It's almost worth having to wear this stupid blazer and the shirt buttoned all the way up to my neck, and the bowtie, and the finger-pointing and the mocking and the silly taunts that I am sure will come as we return home, walking through the middle of town with my mother, at just about the same time as all my school friends are coming out of the cinema.

★

It's 26 July, the day when all of Cuba celebrates the Revolution. It's a public holiday, which is good, and it's the day that Fidel gives the most important speech of the year, which is not so good because it means the cinema is closed and there is nothing on television or the radio except Fidel. Since early in the morning *La Compañera* from the Committee for the Defence of the Revolution has been knocking on doors and stopping people in the street to remind them that *El Maxímo Líder* is speaking tonight, Make sure you tune in, all right? This time I think Fidel speaks for six hours. It feels like six hours, anyway. It's a mystery to a boy my age how anyone can stand up at a lectern in front of hundreds of thousands of people and speak for six hours without notes and without taking a break to go to the toilet. I guess it's a

167

mystery to most Cubans, too, but no one ever seems to comment on this.

My parents say that when Fidel first came down from the mountains and Cuba had lots of capitalist newspapers and lots of game shows on television and soap operas on the radio, Fidel would just walk into the studio at the CMQ television station whenever he wanted. He would interrupt whatever variety show was on and as the leggy, feather-covered dancers disappeared off the studio floor, *El Comandante en Jefe* would speak straight to the cameras, straight to the People, about what was happening on the island. Those speeches must have been entertaining because most Cubans my parents' age recall them with fondness. Even if you didn't have a television set, they say, you would go to the nearest electrical goods shop and stand on the footpath and watch the flickering black and white screens in the shop window, hoping that tonight, like last night, Fidel would again burst into the studio without any notice, interrupt whatever was on and take the rest of Cuba into his confidence.

But tonight it is different because tonight Fidel sounds even more serious than usual, talking about his new idea to fix the Cuban economy once and for all so that we won't have to queue any more for rice and beans and we won't have to carry the ration book and *la jaba*. Fidel says we are going to have the biggest sugar harvest in the history of Cuba. Ever! The 1969 sugar harvest is going to be the sugar harvest to end all sugar harvests—ten million tonnes of sugar will be harvested and shipped to the world. Then, when the money rolls in, we will watch in amazement as the empty shelves in the shops fill up again with all sorts of goods, including not very revolutionary luxuries like toilet paper and shampoo.

Ten million tonnes of sugar is a figure I can barely understand but it sounds like a lot of sugar and all I can think of is that now my parents have applied to leave Cuba, we are going to miss out on all the food and the clothes and the television sets and the washing machines and the Polish refrigerators that Fidel is going to hand out to Cubans on the back of the biggest sugar harvest in the history of the entire world. Trust my parents to pick this time to leave.

Later, much later, historians will say that this one announcement changed the course of the Revolution. For the next twelve months, the island is turned upside down and everyone, absolutely everyone, no matter how old or how young or how frail, is expected to do their bit so we can reach that magical target of ten million tonnes. Even *gusanos* like my father, who is already cutting sugarcane for the Revolution, is expected to work harder and longer. The effort will result in the total collapse of what was left of the Cuban economy but we don't know this now. We still think everything will be just fine.

On television, at the cinema and in the paper—all they talk about is the ten million tonne sugar harvest: *la zafra de los diez millones*. It never stops, and nothing else matters. At school the teachers ditch the regular lessons so they can spend time explaining why the ten million tonne harvest is so important for the Revolution. At the cinema they even have cartoons about the ten million tonne harvest. My favourite is a black and white cartoon in which a funny-looking, wiry man, wearing a big hat like those worn by sugarcane cutters to protect them from the sun and the heat, fills big canvas sacks full of pristine white Cuban sugar. Each sack gets bigger and bigger until the last one is huge and has written on it the slogan every adult and child in Cuba now knows off by heart: *¡Los diez millones van!*, which loosely translates as, The ten million are a done deal.

On the news there are lots of reports about Fidel travelling up and down the island cutting sugarcane with ordinary Cubans, or inspecting ordinary Cubans doing their job and offering hints and advice on how to work faster and better, as only Fidel can do. Billboards on the main road outside Banes carry pictures of Fidel in a big hat and working clothes, cutting sugarcane. There are even songs on the radio about how terrific it is to spend your spare time cutting sugarcane.

The ten million tonnes are so important to the future of Cuba and the future of the Revolution that everyone is expected to do their part. That is why *Granma* has pictures of happy Cubans—people who normally work as doctors, nurses, teachers or mechanics—changing into denim trousers and long-sleeved denim shirts and walking off their job for two or three weeks so they, too, can go and cut sugarcane. There are also lots of pictures of ministers cutting sugarcane with Fidel and pictures of smiling foreigners cutting sugarcane—even important visitors like the Soviet Minister for Defence. There are pictures, too, of young people from Europe and even some from the United States who have come to Cuba to help. I read these stories in the library, where I go to look at the paper and sometimes at *Bohemia* magazine and just to spend some time in a place that is brightly lit, quiet and full of books, and where no one talks about the sugar harvest because if you do, the librarian says, Please, *compañero*, be quiet. This is a library.

The stories in the paper say that these young volunteers have come from across the world to help because with the exception of the hated Richard Nixon with a swastika in his name, the people of the world are all right behind the Revolution. Even young Americans support Fidel, the paper says, and so we welcome them to Cuba to help with *los diez millones*. It makes me feel very good and very Cuban to see so many young people come from everywhere to help. In the pictures in *Granma*, they all look very white and very determined and, to my initial surprise, most of the young men from Europe and from the United States have long hair, which is strange because I always thought this was a sign of capitalism and decadence.

And almost every night, instead of old movies, both television channels will switch to a special report from Fidel in the studio giving a daily account of the harvest. On my friend's socialist television set, you can see *El Comandante en Jefe* standing before a huge map of Cuba, pacing up and down, talking all the time until his voice gets so hoarse from talking he can only whisper. In one hand he has a half-lit cigar and in the other he has a long, thin pointer that he uses again and again, just like my teachers do at school, to show how the production targets are going in different provinces, municipalities and towns. There are six provinces in Cuba and I don't know how many municipalities, so Fidel's report can take a long, long time.

My friend's mother comes in, turns off the television set and says, as mothers do, Time to say goodnight and head off to bed because you have school tomorrow, and so my brother and I go home, and still Fidel keeps talking and talking and talking. I know because as we walk along the street heading for home in the cool of the night, we can still hear Fidel's voice.

Perhaps I am under the influence of my parents' counter-revolutionary skepticism, but sometimes I don't quite understand how all the problems in Cuba will be solved just because we end up with double the amount of sugar that is normally harvested every year. But I keep these thoughts to myself because, let's face it, if Fidel says the harvest will be ten million tonnes then it is pretty much guaranteed that no one anywhere will contradict *El Maxímo Líder* because he *knows* what he is talking about. I heard Fidel on the radio during one of his long speeches saying the ten million tonne harvest would be dedicated to the heroic people of Vietnam, who are fighting

171

the imperialists and their South Vietnamese lackeys. He also said it would be a huge embarrassment for Cuba in the eyes of the rest of the world if we don't meet the ten million tonne target. *Una gran verguenza.*

19 · NO MORE CHRISTMAS FOR YOU

There are lots of good things about the ten million tonne sugar harvest, like the way we don't get to do much work at school because half the teachers are cutting sugarcane in the countryside and those who are left behind are so busy all they do is keep an eye on classes that seem to get more and more rowdy by the day. But there are some bad things about *los diez millones* too, even though no one complains about them. Like the way they have cancelled a lot of television programs so we can watch Fidel's nightly progress reports instead, or the way the cinema is now closed on most weeknights so that the projectionist can do his bit by the Revolution and go and cut sugarcane. And now, Fidel has announced that Christmas is cancelled.

My friends and I can't understand it but it's true. We saw it with our own eyes: Fidel gave a speech in Havana in which he announced that, because of the ten million tonne sugar harvest, we would have to make a small sacrifice and postpone the Christmas holidays. There will be no *Nochebuena* this year. Fidel says Cuba is not a religious country any more and what is the point of celebrating a religious festival that was imported from Europe generations ago? In Europe, it is cold and snowy in December and everyone needs to rest indoors, he says, but not here in tropical Cuba. Here, it is still hot in December even though it's supposed to be our winter and, besides, it's prime sugar harvesting time.

So, Fidel says, standing there behind the lectern, his long fingers caressing the tops of the microphones, we have decided that Christmas will be postponed this year. We will have to save the pork meat for later, and the beans that Cubans use to make *congri*, and the Spanish nougat sweets, and the beer and the rum. Because we will now celebrate six months later—in July, when it's the middle of summer. July 26 will be the new day for Christmas, he says, because in any case, that is the day that commemorates the start of the Revolution; the day in 1953 when Fidel and his brother Raul and a group of other young men attacked the Moncada barracks in Santiago de Cuba. It's already the most important day in the Cuban revolutionary calendar, and now it will be doubly important, Fidel says.

And what a celebration this will be, he tells the crowd, which interrupts his speech with a lot of applause and shouting and anti-American slogans: *Fidel seguro, a los Yankees¡ dales duro!* Fidel, for sure, hit those Yankees hard! Because by July 1970, the ten million tonne harvest will be over and Cubans will have met their revolutionary targets, having squeezed every last pound of sugar from every last acre of sugarcane. Then we will really have something to celebrate, says Fidel to thunderous applause from the audience, which is obviously as confident of success as *El Máximo Líder*.

Everyone on television seems to think it's a great idea to cancel Christmas to help the Revolution but I have my doubts because *Nochebuena* has always been a big family holiday for us,

174

when all of my mother's brothers and sisters and their families and my cousins come to Banes for a big dinner and a big party. Not this year. Everyone will be cutting sugarcane with Fidel on 24 December and on the 25th and even on the 31st. And on New Year's Day, too. There is going to be no *Nochebuena* for anyone, and no Christmas trees either because, Fidel says, they are a silly, antiquated European custom that has no meaning in revolutionary Cuba, where we are all busy building socialism.

What worries me most is not the postponing of *Nochebuena* or the abolition of the Christmas tree but what happens to the Day of the Three Kings, on 6 January. Have I heard this right? Did *El Maxímo Líder* really say that the Revolution will also postpone the Day of the Three Kings? This is the day when children up and down the length of Cuba wake up as early as their parents will allow them and head straight for the Christmas tree, complete with fake snow and coloured lights, to see what toys the Three Wise Men have left for them. *El Día de los Reyes* has been around since colonial days, everyone knows that, and now it looks as if it's being cancelled too. Perhaps I misheard?

I run out of the house and around the corner to see Pepitin, whose family used to own what my mother says was the best pastry shop in all of Banes but which nowadays is only open a couple of hours a day, selling a few biscuits and every now and then a sponge cake, which you are allowed to order with your ration book if there is a birthday in the family. Pepitin is as confused as we all are about *el Día de los Reyes* so we run out of his house and down the street again, this time heading towards the park where we are sure we will find some of the other neighbourhood kids hanging around.

They are there all right but no one seems to know for sure what all this means. It takes a while for everyone to calm down and in the end we agree that, yes, 6 January has been postponed too. Fidel said so. He said that children were the most important people in Cuba and also the luckiest because since the Revolution, every child in Cuba has access to free health care and free education, which is something *El Maxímo Líder* is always reminding us about. In the old days, before the Revolution, only rich children got toys on 6 January while poor children never got anything Fidel says. Now, thanks to the Revolution, every day is a good day for Cuban children, so like the good revolutionaries that we are, like the good communists that we want to be, we will have to wait six months—until 26 July!—to get our presents. Except it will no longer be called *el Día de los Reyes*, but *el Día del Niño*—Children's Day.

It seems like a small price to pay to defend the Revolution, but I am devastated. I suspect all my friends are too, but we don't say much about it. If Fidel says that every day is a great day for Cuban children, then he must know what he is talking about. We are lucky to be Cuban children, says Julito, one of the neighbourhood group, although I suspect he is just repeating what his parents tell him at home, or what his parents tell him to say to his friends if the topic ever comes up. Besides, Julito says, by 26 July the sugar *zafra* will be over and everyone will have so much to celebrate that there will be truckloads of toys arriving in Banes for all of us, the lucky children of the Revolution. We agree, but as I walk back home, I start thinking: what happens if, despite all the work, and despite cancelling *Nochebuena* and abolishing Christmas trees and postponing the Day of the Three Kings, we can't reach the ten million tonnes of sugar? I realise immediately that these are very counter-revolutionary thoughts, even for the son of *gusanos*. They are the type of thoughts you keep to yourself. But I can't help myself, and I am surprised, really, that apart from my father, no one else seems to think that this is even a possibility. No one imagines that the *diez millones* may not come true. Fidel says *los diez millones van* and everyone agrees because that is the way things are in Cuba. No one ever contradicts Fidel.

★

The woman who heads the Committee for the Defence of the Revolution, *La Compañera*, who keeps an eye on everyone and everything in the neighbourhood, has come around to talk to my mother about doing some volunteer work. This doesn't really mean you are invited to volunteer but rather you are told to turn up and do your bit on behalf of the Revolution. In this case, *La Compañera* has told my mother that she is expected tonight and every night for the next few weeks to help sort coffee beans.

In the past, my mother would probably have made some excuse because she says that after a hard day's work at the shop, who wants to go and spend time doing volunteer work that isn't really volunteer work? But things are different now: we have applied to leave Cuba and when you apply to leave Cuba you need a lot of important people to give you the tick before you are allowed out—important people like the president of your local Committee for the Defence of the Revolution. So, this time around, there is no way my mother is going to refuse or arrive late because she knows that if she does, *La Compañera* will put a big black cross instead of a tick next to her name on the list and that's not likely to help us much.

And it's not as if my mother has to go too far from home. The volunteered volunteers will do their bit for the Revolution just a few doors down from our house, on the other side of the street, at the Masonic Centre, a two-storey building that adults would probably describe as elegant, at least by Banes standards. It has shuttered windows upstairs, a covered veranda and columns at the entrance that look like the ones you see in gladiator movies, and the building is surrounded by a high iron fence. To my friends and me this is the most mysterious building in the street, if not in all of town, because no one lives there and you very rarely see anyone going in or out. We have no idea what goes on behind those big, solid doors at the front but it can't be good because you can see as you look up at the second storey that right there, at the top, near the roof, someone has carved what looks like an eye. A single eye, unblinking, watching everything.

I have never been inside the building and neither has any of my friends, which is fine by me because I think it'd probably be quite scary inside too. But I know that some nights small groups of men who seem quite old to my friends and me turn up at the door, knock and go in, and then much later in the night they come out again. One of my older friends says the men who go in are members of a secret society called the Masons, and that once inside, they kill a goat—a sacrifice, my friend says—so they can drink the warm, red blood and live forever, which of course I don't believe for a minute. But the other kids do and on cue everyone makes noises as if they are going to throw up. I try to tell them that if the Masons were really killing a goat inside we would hear the goat squealing really loudly because that is exactly what happens when my father kills a pig at Christmas time: the pig squeals when the knife goes in. I know because I have seen it with my own eyes. None of my friends is even vaguely interested in my explanation.

Once I asked my uncle Rogelio about the Masons and the building and he told me that my uncle Tony, who is now in Havana, used to be a member of the Masons when he was younger, *antes del Triunfo*, when a lot of important people in Banes were all members of the Masons and visited the Masonic Centre all the time. My uncle Rogelio assured me they don't kill goats inside but he warned me, as my mother has, not to even think about jumping the high fence and having a snoop around the place. It's strange how adults can read your mind.

Now my mother has the chance to see for herself what goes on inside the Masonic Centre because *La Compañera* says that the Masons have volunteered the building for volunteer work—and I want to go with her and have a look too, so that I can tell my friends how wrong they are, because I am sure there will be no goats inside, dead or alive. My mother is not the least bit interested but she agrees that I can come with her, provided I help out sorting the coffee beans, which I am happy to do. But when we get there, right after dinner, I find that no one is going to be allowed inside the building. No, no, says *La Compañera*, standing right in front of the locked doors. We are all working out there, *compañeras*, where it is much cooler, she says, pointing to the long table set up on the veranda that faces the street. Now I am stuck here helping my mother. She and about two dozen other women from the street sit at the long table going through huge mountains of unroasted coffee beans, picking out the ones that have gone off or look too ugly and setting them aside. Then they pour the good coffee beans into huge sacks which are taken away somewhere to be roasted and then, I imagine, the good, roasted coffee beans will be sent off to one of the fraternal socialist countries in Eastern Europe so that Russians and Albanians can enjoy Cuban coffee.

My mother keeps shaking her head as she selects the beans because, she says later, while the Russians and the Albanians drink our good Cuban coffee, back here, she says, we are lucky to drink any coffee at all since coffee is strictly rationed. There is never enough coffee, no matter how many times my mother uses the same coffee powder again and again in the *colandera* my father made from canvas cloth. All you get in the end is a cup of brown water. Still, there is a plus from all that coffee work at the Masonic Centre for my mother and the other volunteered women: when they think that *La Compañera* isn't looking, I catch them hiding some of the good coffee beans in their aprons or in their pockets so they can take them home. I am sure *La Compañera* can see them too, but she doesn't say anything. She probably has coffee beans in her pockets too.

Well, my father was right. It's now official: we have failed to harvest ten million tonnes of sugar. *La zafra de los diez millones*, the harvest that turned the country upside down, the harvest that was to deliver Cuba from poverty and scarcity forever, isn't going to happen.

Fidel has been on television and radio, as he is almost every other night, except this time his voice is hoarse even before he starts speaking, and his hair is all over the place. He looks tired and his uniform looks like it needs a good wash. He plays around with the big microphones stuck to the lectern, like he always does, explaining that despite a great revolutionary effort the *zafra* has not gone as well as we expected and we won't make the ten million tonnes, *compañeros*. In fact, he says, we have missed our goal by fifteen per cent. It is still a huge amount of sugar but way short of the target.

It's really bad news—you can tell just by looking at Fidel on the television screen. Halfway through his speech, he tells the crowd below that he is so disappointed about the harvest that he is quite happy to resign as *Comandante en Jefe* if that is what the People want. But just as you would expect, the crowd starts yelling out, No! No! No! and then they start singing the national anthem and chanting, Fidel! Fidel! Fidel!, which means Fidel isn't going anywhere. When Fidel fails, everyone fails. It's what the Revolution is all about.

I think it is probably a mistake: someone must have failed to count all the tonnes carefully and missed a million or two. I can't understand how we could have failed despite mobilising everyone around the country, despite inviting thousands of young people with long hair and very white teeth from Europe and from Canada and even the United States to come to Cuba to cut sugarcane, despite all the time spent on television and radio talking about the *zafra*. The end result is failure just like my father said would happen. Still, it's no cause for celebration in our *gusano* household. My father is still in the countryside and my mother is sure this news can mean only one thing: even longer queues at the shops.

Not that anyone on television or in the papers talks about failure quite that way, of course. They say this is nonetheless a magnificent, revolutionary effort; a record *zafra* that only the Revolution could have delivered. The biggest sugar harvest in Cuban history! No one points out that given the effort involved this is nothing to sing and dance about, especially since all other aspects of the economy have come to a costly standstill while everyone has been cutting sugarcane. It's the lowest point in Fidel's revolutionary experiment thus far, historians outside Cuba will say later, but for now I just try to understand what it means. All I know is what they say in the paper: like good revolutionaries, we must turn failure into victory!

Besides, deep inside, I don't want to admit that my father, who is so cynical about anything to do with the Revolution, could have been so right in his prediction. But he is—and it's not the first time, either. I remember when Fidel announced another one of his big ideas to fix the Cuban economy, the *Cordón de la Habana*, which meant digging up all the gardens and parks and forests around Havana so that volunteer workers could grow a special type of coffee plant. The coffee plants would encircle the city and produce so much coffee Cubans would be able to drink strong, sweet Cuban coffee around the clock—and still export plenty to the rest of the world. Back then, my father said it was a stupid idea because coffee only grows well at high altitude, up in the mountains, no matter what Fidel says. He was right—despite all that work, the coffee bushes refused to produce coffee.

Then, when Fidel announced the ten million tonne sugar harvest last year, I remember my father shaking his head and saying, He is crazy. It will never happen. When I asked him why not, he said that anyone who has ever been near a Cuban cane field or anyone who knows how Cuban transport works (or more accurately, doesn't work) would come to the same conclusion. And I know what I am talking about, he said with a sure tone, because I grew up on a sugarcane farm. All those people who stop working as nurses and teachers and in offices so they can cut sugarcane, well, he says, all they will do is get in the way of the real cane-cutters, the professional *macheteros*. You will see, he says to me . . .

What I can't understand now is if my father, a simple *guajiro* from Banes, knew from the very start that ten million tonnes was a crazy target—even if you stretch cutting time by six months!—why didn't anyone in Havana tell Fidel? Why did they let *El Comandante en Jefe* make those promises in the first place? Why did they let Fidel dedicate the ten million tonnes of sugar to the heroic Vietnamese people? My father has an explanation for that too: he says Fidel doesn't listen to anyone. When he gets a big idea, no one can stop him. Well, this time at least, before he made any announcement he should have driven to Banes in his olive green jeep and talked to my *guajiro* father because my *guajiro* father was right. Dead right.

Everyone I come across at school, at the Parque Cardenas, sitting near the steps on the corner, seems to be totally deflated and confused. After so much work and so many promises, we are back to square one. And the worst thing of all is that when 26 July comes along in a few weeks, when we are supposed to be celebrating the new, revolutionary *Nochebuena*, there will be nothing much to celebrate. And when the new, revolutionary equivalent of *el Día de los Reyes* is finally here, we will probably end up getting no toys or only very crappy toys because now that there is no *zafra de los diez millones*, where is Fidel going to get the money to buy all those toys he promised to the children of the Revolution?

I should not have worried so much—there will still be Children's Day and this year it will be held in July as expected and, yes, we are all going to get toys, not from the Three Wise Men like we used to, but from Fidel, who is also very wise. But first, we will have to queue to get them. That is where I am right now, queuing with my mother and my brother at the only toy shop left in Banes, near my parents' old shop, the one that no longer exists.

It's a long queue, like all queues in Cuba, and while we wait and wait and wait my mother talks to some of the other mothers in the line, trying to make sense of the new rules for buying toys that have just been announced in the paper. You can buy toys only if you have children and you need your ration book because toys are strictly rationed too. Fidel says this is so each child can get toys for Children's Day: a basic toy—*juguete básico*—which is the biggest and most expensive you can spot when it is your turn at the counter, and one non-basic toy which is smaller and less popular.

Of course, all the really good basic toys disappear quickly, so that whoever is first in line will usually get the biggest prize—

the one Chinese-made bicycle in the whole shop, complete with a fancy bell and plastic tassels hanging from the handlebar and even a basket for your school books. When it's our turn to choose, having finally made it into the toy shop, the selection is already a little limited, which is a problem not just for me but for the twenty or thirty families still lined up behind us, anxiously awaiting their turn.

I look around the half-empty shelves but there is not much of a choice, as I feared, until I see it, right there near the till: a yellow-coloured dumper truck with big rubber wheels. I can tell it's a good toy and not only because it says on the box that it is made in Japan. It feels solid and forbiddingly capitalist. There is only one problem, says my mother: batteries. She is right—it is a battery-powered truck and batteries are very hard to come by in Cuba. You never see them in the shops. There isn't even a space in the ration book for batteries, that's how rare they are. You know what will happen when the batteries that come in the box run out, don't you? I can hear my mother saying. I know, I reply, I know what will happen but I don't care because I want the yellow-coloured, Japanese-made, battery-powered dumper truck and nothing she says will dissuade me from choosing this as my basic toy.

Do I need to tell you my mother was right? The batteries in the box lasted a day even though I was careful not to waste them by playing with the truck too much. I swear. I never saw batteries in Cuba again. At least that wasn't a problem with my non-basic toy: a box of colouring pens made in Hungary.

I have no idea what toys the families who were at the very end of the queue managed to get because I am sure there wasn't much left by the time they made it to the counter. I know there were lots of not very happy children in Banes, and probably all over Cuba, and a lot of not very happy mothers and fathers who had to put up with their not very happy children. So many not happy families that Fidel announced that a new, more revolutionary, much fairer system would be introduced next year: a lottery to be organised by the Committees for the Defence of the Revolution in each *barrio* to decide which lucky family in the neighbourhood would be first in the toy queue . . . and get the best toys.

20 · WE WANT TO BE LIKE CHE!

I am now in secondary school—my last year of school in Cuba, as it will turn out. I am enrolled in a school that is now known as Heroes de Playa de Girón, which is the name Cubans use to refer to what everyone else in the world knows as the Bay of Pigs invasion. With impeccable revolutionary irony, the school that now celebrates what the newspaper calls the First Ever Defeat of American Imperialism in the Western Hemisphere used to be an American-owned school run by American Quakers. According to my mother, it was by far the best school in town, modelled on some American college in South Dakota or Illinois, complete with ovals, a baseball diamond and a walkway going all the way down to a creek just behind the school grounds. The classrooms are light and airy with expansive windows looking out on what once must have been a manicured American-style garden but is now little more than a patch of neglected brown Cuban dirt.

Going to secondary school means you get to make new friends and meet new teachers but, best of all, it means I am now old enough to take part in *escuela al campo*, which my mother says

186

is a crazy new revolutionary experiment designed to indoctrinate children—that's the word she uses!—to hate their parents. I am sure she is exaggerating. It means that every year secondary schools close down for a fortnight and the whole school— teachers, students, blackboards, everything—is moved to the countryside, to a camp that is a cross between a military base and a summer holiday spot for inquisitive and overactive adolescents. Now, how good is that? I can't wait to pack my things. To my mother, however, it's nothing short of a tragedy. She is losing her son to the Revolution and she is beside herself.

As our school principal explains it, we will get some lessons but much of the day will be spent helping the Revolution by picking lemons. Lemons are important, the principal says, because the Revolution can then export juicy, tart Cuban lemons to our friends in Eastern Europe in exchange for things we need in Cuba, like harvesters and tractors and petrol. I think we need lemons in Cuba too as we never see them in the shops, but I decide there is no need to be a smarty-pants. And you never know how your teachers will take such a comment or whether it will end up in your *expediente escolar*, the file every school child in Cuba accumulates. It is supposed to detail everything you do and everything you say, including things you shouldn't have said. Anyway, I am excited about this whole *escuela al campo* business, even if my mother is mortified, thinking of ways she can stop the inevitable from happening.

The camp we are going to is at Punta de Mulas, or Mules Point, which is not all that far from Banes, probably an hour or so by road. Everyone at school is going—all the teachers and all the students—even though in theory it is not compulsory. It's never made clear what would happen if you or your parents decided not to do your bit for the Revolution and refused to go to *la escuela al campo*. As far as I know, no one says no unless you are really sick and can get a certificate from your doctor or the local polyclinic. I am sure my mother has thought of that too, but in the end there is no choice: I am off to the school in the countryside. I can kind of understand why my mother is so distraught—my father is already in the countryside cutting sugarcane and now her eldest son is off to the countryside too, leaving her and my brother back home alone. My mother misses my father, like my brother and I do, and now . . . *Mira, mira*, she says to one of my aunts, pointing at me *¡si es un niño!* Look, he is only a boy! I don't think she understands what Fidel says about how Cuba is building a New Man.

The morning we are to leave for the *escuela al campo* there are several Russian-made military trucks parked at Parque Cárdenas waiting to take us to the camp. The trucks are like those I have seen in Russian movies about the Great Patriotic War, except someone has removed the canvas tops so we can all stand on the back and wave goodbye to our parents—or in my case, just to my mother and brother, who has been carrying on for days because he, too, wants to go to the countryside instead of having to stay behind as though he is a baby, which he is not.

Like most of my fellow students, I have a *mochila* that is huge, packed with school books, bedsheets, clothes, a tin or two of food my mother has managed to find somewhere (I never ask where or how), an enamel plate and mug and a pair of boots for all the hard work ahead picking lemons. As we line up to have our names crossed off, I can see a hundred mothers anxiously watching as their children clamber up onto the back of the truck. We are all so excited you can barely hear anything above the shouting and the laughing and the singing.

It's true that we will only be a few kilometres from home but for my mother and the other mothers standing at the edge of the park, waving and shouting at their kids to take care and don't forget to take your medicine, it is like we are being sent to Jupiter. There are no buses from Banes to Punta de Mulas. In fact, there is barely any transport at all and the road is not much more than a dirt track in some parts, so visiting will be an absolute nightmare for our families. As the trucks start pulling out I wave goodbye to my mother, who is now holding my brother's hand tightly, I can tell. She is about to cry and I am embarrassed by her tears, thinking, How could she? Doesn't she know I am a big boy now? But then when I look around the truck I realise that it's gone quiet all of a sudden and that there are some first year girls—and even boys—wiping away tears as they wave goodbye.

As soon as we leave the park someone starts singing some revolutionary song and everyone joins in like the good little communists that we are. Then the revolutionary songs give way to Spanish pop songs we sometimes hear on the radio and, before we know it, the trucks are out in the countryside, the road is bumpy and in the distance I can see row after row after row of lemon trees, heavy with small green and yellow Cuban lemons. There must be hundreds of trees, all in neat rows, and it hits me that picking lemons for the Revolution is not going to be as much fun as most of us on the back of the truck expected.

When we finally arrive at the camp, we drive through two large gates and see a number of what look like long, squat military barracks joined to rooms that look like classrooms which are in turn joined to a central area which, I assume, is where the kitchen and the dining room are located. It's not what you'd describe as homely but then again I don't think anyone thought it would be.

We are told to jump out of the trucks and line up quickly and without such a racket, *compañeros*, so that we can be assigned to our brigades, which will become a kind of surrogate extended family for the next two weeks. Then we are shown to the barracks where we are assigned bunk beds. Some barracks are for boys while others are for girls, with teachers sleeping in the middle, supposedly to keep an eye on older students who may get a little adventurous when it comes to sleeping arrangements. This is not something that even crosses my mind initially but I know that some of the older boys at school have been talking about the endless opportunities ahead to spend time with the opposite sex. As I will discover, they are right.

For the duration we are to follow what is probably supposed to be a strict, military-style regime intended, no doubt, to teach us how to become good revolutionaries like Che. However, in typically Cuban fashion, it seems more like a very disorganised, half-hearted attempt at an enforced holiday than anything else, at least for now, with teachers sending kids to the wrong barracks and backpacks getting lost and one or two of the younger girls still crying because, well, I think they miss their mothers.

Once we have been allocated bunk beds and shown where the showers and the latrines are we have to line up again for the teachers to select the students who will be the brigade leaders, a job that will involve not just ensuring everyone behaves but that everyone works hard enough for the brigade to meet its production target. The brigade that meets its targets most consistently by picking the most lemons will be awarded a certificate, just like the certificates that are awarded on television by Fidel or Raul to the best workers to recognise their outstanding contribution to building socialism in the tropics. There are no other prizes, of course, because this is socialist Cuba and in socialist Cuba we are building the New Man and, just like Che, the New Man doesn't want or need material goods to be a good revolutionary.

To my surprise, I hear my name called out. I have been selected as leader of my brigade, a group of about ten students, some much older than I am but obviously way less committed to picking lemons for the Revolution. Being chosen a brigade leader is like getting a huge revolutionary star on your forehead, or like being the biggest teacher's pet in the entire universe. When I think about it later, I realise than I am more relieved than excited at my new-found important role as a *dirigente*, a revolutionary leader in the making. I am relieved at the fact that I haven't been excluded. I was dead-set convinced I would not be chosen for such an important revolutionary job because, well, you know, my ungrateful parents want to leave Cuba and take me away with them. And who ever heard of a brigade leader being the son of *gusanos*? Yes, I know why my parents say they want to leave Cuba and I know that it's for the best and all that stuff they have told us over and over again at home, but for now, I am thrilled with my new promotion. I want to be a good Cuban, which means I want to be a good revolutionary, which means I want to be like Che!

In the mornings we are woken up by one of the students playing his bugle. We wash in communal bathrooms, change into our work clothes and file in for breakfast in the huge central dining room, before assembling outside to raise the flag and listen to the school principal explain just how lucky we are to live in a society where every child has the right to go to school which, he adds, was not the case *antes del Triunfo*. Full of revolutionary fervour, we line up and march off into the distance, down the dirt roads around camp to where the lemon groves are, to spend the morning picking lemons for the Revolution.

The work seems easy at first but it gets harder and more tedious as the day progresses. The thorns of the lemon trees appear to have no problem piercing through the gloves we have been given so that before long, if you aren't careful, your hands end up a bloody mess. The long-sleeved shirts offer only limited protection against the sun, which is getting hotter and hotter by the minute as we pick lemon after lemon after lemon. We carry the big wooden boxes full of lemons to trucks parked along a central trail, and these trucks take the lemons to a warehouse somewhere for further distribution. At least I hope so. This being Cuba, there is a sneaking suspicion among some of my wiser and older school mates that those lemons we have just picked with such revolutionary determination for our friends in Prague and Warsaw and Budapest may well end up staying in the warehouse until they rot because there are no spare parts to fix the trucks or because someone, somewhere, failed to fill in the necessary forms.

Some afternoons the teachers attempt to conduct regular classes, without much success, and then at about five or six o'clock we are allowed time to have a shower and change into clean clothes, but not before we all line up again to get our names crossed off. There may be no wire fences around the camp and no armed guards but there are very strict rules about leaving the camp. Some afternoons we also march in military style or learn how to disassemble and clean rifles, how to load an ancient-looking machine gun and how to shoot at targets because, as we are told every day and reminded every night, we must be prepared to defend the Revolution *con nuestra propia sangre*—with our own blood.

We have also been taught how to make our beds and fold our sheets as if we were in the army, how to polish our boots like an army sergeant, how to stand to attention and how to line up in military style in front of our bunks for inspection. It's good to know that if those Yankee invaders ever arrive on our shores, we will be ready with our clean rifles, our spotless boots and our bedsheets folded just so. We then have dinner in the large dining hall where we queue for our food and a glass of water.

The food is plentiful but uniformly tasteless: there is nothing on offer for the whole fortnight but boiled rice and a kind of stew made from canned Russian sausages that are a funny pink colour and that pretty much taste like cardboard, and not very good cardboard at that. Then, after dinner, the camp comes alive. Almost every night there is a show put on by one of the brigades—each takes turn to perform and while some try to take it all seriously and read revolutionary poems by the Chilean poet Pablo Neruda or sing revolutionary *campesino* songs written by Carlos Puebla, in the end, most nights, it's just good Cuban fun with good Cuban music. Then we are all sent to bed, the lights are turned off, and the barracks fall silent. At least that's the way it looks to me.

Some days later, after dinner, I talk to a boy in my brigade who is in second year and whose nickname is *El Sapo*—the toad—although I never call him that to his face because he is older and taller and stronger than I am, even if he is not all that bright: he has had to repeat second year twice. We are both in the kitchen, scrubbing the huge black pots that are used to cook the rice, because tonight it's my brigade's turn to help with the washing up. *El Sapo*, who will never win an award for being an exemplary student—*un estudiante ejemplar*—but who seems to know so much more than I do when it comes to girls, says that all the action happens right after dark, once the lights are out. I have no idea what kind of action he is talking about but I keep quiet because I don't want to sound as though I am an ignorant first year student who doesn't know anything.

When all of you are in bed asleep, says *El Sapo*, and when the teachers disappear from sight, *chico*, that is when things get hot out there. *Caliente*, he says and he winks. If you believe him, the teachers are always catching couples kissing behind the barracks and doing other things, he says mysteriously, making a rude Cuban sign with his forefinger. Only the other night, he says, they caught a male teacher with one of the older girl students, kissing near the showers. True, he says, all hell broke lose: ¡*Tremendo escándalo!* But then they just hushed it up and sent the teacher back to Banes and the girl was told to keep quiet or she'd be in real trouble.

I don't know whether I believe *El Sapo* or not. The fact that he is still in second year when he should be in fourth makes me think he is not the smartest boy at school but then again, why would he want to impress me with his stories? I decide it doesn't matter. I am too tired, anyway, and I know that tomorrow morning we will line up again and set off to pick more lemons for the Revolution. All I want to do is go to bed. As I drift off to sleep that night, I can see a long conga line of sun-ripened lemons, full of juice and surrounded by thorns, calling my name . . .

Sundays are the best days of all at Punta de Mulas. On Sundays we don't have to pick lemons; instead, we get to sleep in until eight, or even later if you don't mind missing breakfast and if you can sleep with all the noise from the other boys in the barracks. Sunday is the official visiting day and by the time we finish breakfast dozens of mothers and fathers and brothers and sisters have arrived at the gates in trucks that have been organised by the school from Banes. Not all the parents come in the trucks. Some come in olive green army jeeps like the ones Fidel sometimes uses when he is visiting *campesinos*. If your parents come in a jeep you know they must be important communists because most people in Banes don't have jeeps. Most people come on the trucks, like my mother.

On Sundays, without fail, my mother arrives because she misses her boy and because she worries, as I knew she would, that her boy is not eating enough. Look at you, she says while she hugs me, look at you! So skinny . . . and you have caught a cold. I can tell! She has with her a huge *jaba* full of food she has cooked at home, probably the result of exchanging one of her old dresses or a pair of leather shoes for some rice and flour and, most amazing of all, some pork fat for frying. *Manteca.*

I am happy to see my mother but I am also a little embarrassed by all the food she has brought, especially when I look around and see that not every mother has had quite the same level of success as mine in finding little treats for their boys and girls. In fact, I can see that some students don't have visitors at all, which makes me feel like a very spoilt child, very bourgeois even, which I know is not something Che would have approved of so I change the subject and tell my mother that I have been made leader of my brigade.

Her smile disappears and is replaced by a look of absolute terror. Leader of your brigade? What does it mean? I explain and she says quietly, I hope they are not telling you that you should disobey your parents and stay behind in Cuba? Are they indoctrinating you? she asks. I can't understand why she has gone all serious like this but I tell her, No, no one is telling me to stay in Cuba, which is not strictly true because at least one of my teachers has said in passing what a shame it is for a smart, studious boy like me, a boy who obviously wants to be a good revolutionary, to be taken out of Cuba. But I don't tell my mother that because she already has plenty to worry about.

Once my mother leaves in the afternoon, I carefully pack up the goodies she has brought and put them under my bunk bed, covering them with one of the spare towels. Later, I will share some of the cake with my friends and they will share some of their stuff with me, but for now, I don't feel like company because I don't want any of my friends to know that I am homesick. So I sit on my own in a grassy area near the dining hall doing nothing, just watching a big, bright Cuban sun slowly turn into a radiant pink and then explode into the colour of blood before it disappears beyond the horizon. When you leave Cuba, I can hear someone in my head saying, you will never see such a sunset again.

My mother even visits a couple of times during the week, hitching a ride with the mother of my friend Fidelito in her still-shiny American car. Midweek visits are allowed but not encouraged, which is just as well as every time my mother comes she says I am too skinny and that I am catching a cold, and every time she departs she cries a little and tells me how I must eat all my food—even the Russian sausages—because I am too skinny and skinny is not good. I wish she wouldn't make such a fuss and treat me like a little child in front of the other kids from my brigade but deep down I know I wouldn't exchange these visits for anything, especially when you can tell that some kids don't get any visitors at all and spend their Sundays in their bunks, reading or pretending to read, or volunteering to help clean the dormitories, or help sweep the dining hall—anything as long as it keeps them busy.

My mother doesn't tell me this but once during my time in the *escuela al campo* she walked all the way from Banes because there was no truck, no *carreta* and certainly no olive green army jeep to take her to the camp at Punta de Mulas. It must have taken her three or four hours, carrying the heavy *jaba* with the food she had prepared. But she never tells me this, not until many, many years later. When she does, I feel terrible.

Something is up, I am sure of it. We just had word that my father is coming back to Banes. He has been away for nearly three years, since the day after the police arrived at our place to confirm that we were now, officially, *gusanos*. Since then my father has spent time in labour camps all over Oriente province, patiently waiting for permission to leave. He has been sent from camp to camp, along with hundreds of other ungrateful *gusanos*, but he has never been sent to a camp anywhere near Banes. Now, out of the blue, the news has arrived that he is being transferred to work just outside Banes and we couldn't be happier. My mother says the fact that my father is being sent to a camp on the outskirts of Banes can mean only one thing: *el telegrama*—that magical telegram that says, yes, you are now free to leave—cannot be all that far away.

Of course, he will still have to work hard during the day but at night he will be able to walk home and have dinner with us and sleep in his own bed. Not only is he going to be close to home but he will not have to cut any more sugarcane, at least not for a while. Instead, the camp he is being sent to is a carpentry shop where they make useful things like windows and doors and huge yokes for the oxen that are still used in the Cuban countryside to till the earth. My father says that compared to cutting sugarcane every day of the week and having to eat the worst food you can imagine, the new place is like a luxury hotel, even if the *milicianos* are in charge and they still carry guns. We just can't believe our luck.

It will be good to have my father home every night so we can get back to something that at least resembles normal life—like it used to be before we decided to seek permission to leave Cuba. Then my mother can stop worrying so much about her absent, skinny husband, although I am sure she will find something else to worry about. And once more I will be able to talk to him about school, even though he says that all we get taught is communist propaganda. Best of all, I want to see my father walk out onto the small front porch of our house on Flor Crombet Street every evening, sit in one of the rocking chairs that have seen better days and then light up the cigars he always keeps aside for after dinner, filling the air with blue smoke and the aroma of Cuba.

★

Our small, paved yard has become a pigsty. Literally. Now that my parents are sure the magic telegram giving us permission to leave Cuba cannot be too far away, my father has exchanged some of his old shirts with a *campesino* he knows outside town for a piglet. It's pink and loud and you can't help thinking of it as a new family pet even though both my brother and I know very well what its ultimate fate will be. This is Cuba. This is a pig. This is food. My father says, Don't get too attached, boys, because we want to fatten the pig and then, when the telegram arrives . . . We know what will happen when the telegram arrives. My father will get the biggest knife in the house and he will kill the pig and we will cook the food, share some of it with our family and take the rest in old, tightly closed biscuit tins to Havana so we can have something to eat while we wait to fly out.

I understand the logic but I still think it's a cruel fate for the poor pig, which stupidly just keeps eating and getting fatter and fatter so that whenever my uncle Papi visits he can't help looking out the window and saying something like, *¡Coño!*, that pig is looking better every day. As the pig keeps making more and more of a mess of what used to be our backyard, I try to tell it that its days are numbered. The telegram will arrive and you will be gone, pig. But pigs can't understand humans, so our pig keeps eating and making a mess of the yard and getting fatter, no matter what I tell it.

21 · THE MAGICAL TELEGRAM

It's here. The telegram that says we can leave Cuba has arrived, and now we have just three days to kill the pig (he must weigh a tonne by now), pack up our things (it won't take long, says my mother), say goodbye to the family and friends and get our bus tickets to Havana. Most important of all, we need to ensure our paperwork is in order.

Our passports have been safely stored for three years, with their prized Spanish visas which take a whole page inside, complete with colourful stamps and seals and the extravagant signature of the Spanish consul in Havana, a signature so showy and elegant-looking, it can only be the signature of a capitalist functionary. By contrast, the most important of all the papers we need to be allowed out of Cuba is a simple, one-page letter written in pencil, with at least a couple of spelling errors, from the commander of the labour camp where my father has spent the last few months. The letter, which is known as *la carta de la agricultura*, confirms that my father has worked long enough and hard enough to be allowed to leave. It's the sort of letter you guard as if it was the most treasured of possessions, which in a way it most certainly is. Without it, you are going nowhere.

The police have come and taken stock of all our goods, which now belong to the People. In reality, we don't have all that much that is valuable but that does not deter the very efficient *milicianos* from going through their checklist with great care, making sure every single plate and every single glass is accounted for. I can tell it's a difficult experience for my parents even though the most senior of the officers, who is known to my father, is very polite, making occasional small talk. The *milicianos* have seen the pig in the backyard and they are curious, which makes me nervous because perhaps the pig also belongs to the Revolution and one of the police officers will turn around to my father and demand to know what the pig is doing in what used to be our backyard but is now a pigsty—and how did it get there, *compañero*? Luckily for us but not so luckily for the pig, they ignore it because the pig wasn't included in the original stocktake of nearly three years ago. The Revolution works in strange ways.

Once the stocktake is over, *La Compañera* from the Committee for the Defence of the Revolution comes to check that everything is in order, no doubt thinking to herself, you can never trust those *gusanos*. Packing up isn't much of a problem. The instructions from the *milicianos* are clear: you can only take personal effects, like your clothes and your toothbrush and a towel. The rest stays behind because, *compañero, esto es propiedad del Pueblo*. All this, comrade, belongs to the People now. I still can't imagine who would want my old shoes or the singlets that my mother has washed so many times the material has become as thin as the skin of an onion, but I am not about to argue. Soon we are standing outside the house, our suitcases packed and ready. It's only then that the finality of what has just happened starts to sink in.

We are to spend our last night in Banes at my aunt Adelina's house before catching the bus to Havana in the morning, but we can't leave until a senior Communist Party functionary arrives to officially 'seal' the house. It's a peculiar ritual this sealing of the house. As we stand outside mingling with the more curious of our neighbours, the official sent by the Party will lock the door and then place a seal across it, declaring that no one can go in or out of the house without permission. I don't know whether there is someone in the local party whose job it is to seal the houses of *gusanos* but if there is then he must have been sick or busy because the official who comes to seal our house turns out to be my uncle Papi, my mother's youngest brother and without doubt the one she feels the closest to. As she is fond of saying, she practically raised him following the death of my grandmother when my uncle was barely in his teens. Now here he is, a senior official in the local Communist Party, locking the front door and sealing our house.

He doesn't say much but it's quite clear to my parents that this wasn't his idea. One of his superiors must have ordered him, my father says later, and you can tell that my uncle feels as uncomfortable as my parents. My mother can't believe her eyes but she says nothing because she knows that there is nothing much she can do. When he is finished, my uncle Papi says, I will see you later, and then he goes back to work. We pick up our cases and walk down the street and then up the hill to my aunt Adelina's house, waving goodbye to people along the way. Some of them stop briefly to have a quick, furtive chat and wish us luck in Spain. *¡Que les vaya bien!* I hope it all goes well. Good luck.

Over dinner, my mother worries about my uncle. It's not the first time they have done this to him, she says. When my aunt Mirta left Cuba, he was called to a special meeting of the local cadres—*los dirigentes del Partido*—and asked to explain why his sister was leaving Cuba.

Up until now, I thought that leaving Banes would be straightforward, at least for me. After all, we have been waiting for this moment for a long time and now, finally, we are on our way, although in Cuba you can never be sure because at any time someone, somewhere, may decide to keep you back for just a little while longer—or forever, if they want to. My father, who has become quite a pessimist, keeps saying we must do everything right. By the book. No surprises, no jumping around with joy, no provocations of any type because we want to make sure we get on that Iberia plane in a few days' time.

I know that what is really worrying him is my aunt Nidia, my totally unpredictable, totally crazy aunt Nidia, who is leaving Cuba with us as part of our *nucleo familiar*. You never know what she is up to. My mother, on the other hand, is too busy worrying about her other sister, the sister she is leaving behind, my aunt Adelina, and about her brothers, especially my uncle Papi. She doesn't say so but I know what she is thinking—that she is deserting her family.

We spend our last day in Banes saying goodbye to as many people as we can, mainly our family, and we do it quietly—no fanfare—because we don't want to tempt fate. My father is busy trying to secure five tickets on the daily bus that travels from Banes to Havana. My aunt Adelina and my uncle Rogelio are coming to Havana, strictly speaking not to farewell us, you understand, but because my uncle needs to see a specialist, or at least that is the excuse. My aunt Mary, who is heavily pregnant, is coming too with my cousin Karina, who is just six, and my cousin Carlitos, who is four, but my uncle Papi is staying in Banes, as we expected, because he is busy at work, though I can tell that even if he wasn't busy, it would not be wise for a man in his position to travel to Havana to farewell his *gusano* sister. My mother would have convinced him not to, I am sure.

I find it hard to say goodbye to my friends in the neighbourhood. Not because I am getting teary or anything like that—no, no, Cuban men don't cry. It's hard because it all seems so . . . final? There is no coming back—everyone says so, even the *milicianos*, and saying goodbye like this, well, it's as though you are being sent into the farthest corner of space, as though you are a tropical version of Yuri Gagarin, except that your rocket just doesn't have enough fuel to return to base. Something like that.

As I say goodbye to my friends, one by one, I make sure I write down their addresses and I promise to write, of course. I will write to tell them about Spain and bullfights and about the latest music and films in Spain and Europe, and about what things are like outside Cuba. I promise them that inside each envelope I will hide a tablet of chewing gum too, because you can't buy chewing gum in Cuba, no matter how good a revolutionary you are.

Despite my best efforts, I get a little teary after all, but just a little, when our two neighbours from the big house right across the street, Fabiola and her sister Ibis, come to say goodbye later that evening. They must be close to fifty, I am sure, and they have lived across from us—from what used to be our house but isn't any more—for as long as anyone can remember, if not longer. They are both teachers, neither has ever married, which my mother says is a great shame because they are such wonderful, educated women and, you know, they come from a family that was well off in Banes—*bien acomodada*. To my brother and me, they are like family.

They know all about farewells like this too, because while both have decided they will stay put in their family home here in Banes, already they have said goodbye to at least one of their brothers and his wife and daughters, who are now living in Spain, and who have promised to be waiting for us. And so I hug Fabiola first and longest because she has always been my favourite but it is Ibis who surprises me most by giving me a goodbye kiss and a hug, and telling me that I should study hard and respect my parents and look after my brother and help them in our new life. Then she says, *No te olvides de tu patria*—Don't forget your homeland.

★

The coach trip between Banes and Havana can take anywhere between fifteen hours and forever. This is not because of the traffic—there is almost none on the highway, only army trucks and jeeps. It all depends on the coach. Some of the coaches that travel long distances from Oriente province to Havana are new ones imported from one of the fraternal communist nations of Eastern Europe. They are big and shiny and noisy and I can picture in my mind one of these socialist coaches sliding elegantly along some super-modern road outside Prague or East Berlin. But here in tropical Cuba, the socialist coaches are always breaking down because of the heat, so that the fifteen-hour trip to Havana can turn into a 24-hour trip or even longer, with passengers jumping out to wait by the side of the road, under an unforgiving sun, for a local mechanic to come along and do his best to fix the problem, or for someone in the next big town to agree to send a replacement coach.

Luckily for us, we are not on one of these new socialist coaches. We are travelling instead in an old American-made coach that has seen better days. Strangely, though, the old American coaches don't break down as often as the Eastern European ones. Just as well. I can see that my mother is becoming increasingly

204

distraught as we say goodbye, first to Banes, then to the small villages that surround it on a trip that we all know is definitively one way.

Back in the mid 1950s, before he married my mother, my father was a conductor on this same bus route but he tells me they were very different days. Back then, being part of the crew of a sparkling new, silver-coloured, air-conditioned American coach was a pretty glamorous job, especially for a young, good-looking man like me, he says with a smile that is meant to make my mother smile too. Every time I went out in my conductor's uniform, he adds with a wink, the girls used to chase me down the streets! My mother, who has heard these stories before, just rolls her eyes upwards and goes back to looking out the windows.

The coach normally stops along the way a few times to refuel and so the passengers can buy a sandwich for lunch, if they are lucky, and stretch their legs. Within a couple of hours of leaving Banes, the first big stop is at Holguin, which is the much bigger town where my father used to live and where several of his brothers still live. And sure enough, at the station we spot my uncle Gerardo, who is even taller and skinnier than my father, waving anxiously. He always reminds me of the kind of silent, tough cowboy you see in old American westerns at the Teatro Hernández.

It's not a long stop so my uncle gives everyone a big hug and kisses my mother and tells my brother and me to be good boys because, after all, we are going on a plane and despite his age he has never been on one of those new jets. He hasn't even been outside Cuba! And don't forget to write, he says to me. Then he gives my father a bundle of his best cigars and says, It's not much, you know, but here is a little something for you to remember your brothers back home, in Cuba.

My father, who pretends he is not the emotional type because this is Cuba and, as I have told you, Cuban men are never emotional, shakes his head and says, No, no, how can I take your cigars? They are so hard to come by. But my uncle Gerardo insists and so my father takes them and I am sure that no matter what he says, he is getting emotional.

22 · HAVANA, *MI AMOR*

This is only my third trip to Havana and, once again, as the Banes coach nears the big capital city I am overawed by the sheer size of the place. I look out of the window of the old American coach to see streets swarming with people, walking, or just chatting on corners, or standing in queues that are much longer than the ones in Banes, waiting outside *bodegas* and cinemas or at bus stops for buses that may or may not arrive. I sense that this is one of those indelible mental pictures I will take with me when we finally fly out on our way to Madrid—a whole city, a whole country of people standing in line, waiting, waiting, waiting . . .

In Havana, we stay not at my uncle Victor's apartment in Miramar as we did on our first visits, but in a neighbourhood called—appropriately enough, says my father—Reparto Mañana. For reasons that are not clear to me, one of our relatives, Olmer, who is a university student, has the keys to this big, empty house that I am assuming must have belonged to some *gusano* at some stage but now belongs to the People—or at least to someone who has in turn loaned it to Olmer for a few days.

It's a good thing we are only expecting to stay in Havana for three or four nights because this is not much of a house, or so we discover as soon as we open the front door. In fact, there is very little inside: a couple of fold-out beds, three or four old wooden chairs, some plates and forks and an old table. In a corner there is a bench seat from an old American car and my father points it out to me and says, This is going to be your *special* bed! He stresses the word special to make it sound exciting, I am sure, but he can tell I am not too impressed. My mother isn't impressed either, although she doesn't say anything.

The place is depressing no matter how much my father tries to make it sound like an adventure, but we all know that it is the best we can do and it's only for a couple of nights. And thank you, thank you, Olmer, you are a great *muchacho*, letting us stay in this place, this empty place, when there is really no other place to stay in. Because you know, *gusanos* can't just turn up at the Hotel Nacional or the Habana Libre Hotel and say, Good evening, sir, we are *gusanos* from Banes and we want to rent a room. Thank you, Olmer.

My uncle Tony is overseas as a member of a delegation to Moscow and in any case there is no way either of my parents would have asked him to let us stay in his apartment because it is tiny. My uncle Victor, who is a big shot in the Revolutionary Armed Forces, who has his own car and who lives in the large apartment in Miramar where the rich used to live *antes del Triunfo*, has made it known to my mother that he has no room at his place this time. We can't stay there, he told my mother, which she understands fully because if anyone found out he had *gusanos* staying at his place, even family members, he would be in trouble. My father is not quite as understanding. He is angry because how can there be no room in such a big place, he wants to know, when we have to stay here in this place and my sons have to sleep on old car seats so they wake up in the morning with sore necks and flea bites on their arms?

My father is right about one thing—we don't spend any time in the house during the day. As soon as it's daylight we get up, have something to eat from the box of food my mother brought on the bus all the way from Banes, and then we go out to visit my cousin Eddi. She is my father's niece, one of his favourites, and she and her husband Orlando have agreed to let us stay at their apartment during the day and even have lunch there if we want to. This is no small favour and my parents are grateful beyond words. They warn my brother and me to make sure we don't tell anyone we are *gusanos* about to leave Cuba for Spain. Using his stern voice, my father says, If anyone asks, we are cousins from Oriente province. We are visiting our relatives. Understood? Understood, we reply.

I don't mind lying this time, especially when my father explains that my cousin's husband is not your average Habanero. Orlando is a captain in the Revolutionary Navy, which means he is almost certainly a member of the Communist Party. Someone on the way up. I can't figure out why he has agreed to let us stay in his house, even if it is only during the daytime, given his position. If anyone found out, he too would have some explaining to do, just like my uncle Victor. And yet here we are, grateful *gusanos* from Banes, having lunch in his home as if it was the most normal thing in the world, which I guess it might be in some countries but not here in Cuba.

Every day Orlando comes home from work in his navy uniform bringing with him plenty of food for everyone, making my mother very happy, as well as plenty of beer and rum, which makes my father very happy. Every afternoon before dinner, I can see him and my father sitting outside the apartment on a little balcony overlooking the street, having a cold beer and talking about I don't know what.

It's something my uncle Victor was not prepared to do, my father says. I know it hurts my mother that she is here in Havana about to leave Cuba forever and she still has not been able to see and say goodbye to her oldest brother. These are not happy days for my mother and sometimes I wonder whether at some stage she is going to say to my father, No, I am not going to Spain. I am staying here. I can't leave the rest of my family behind. But she doesn't and I am glad she doesn't because if she did, I really have no idea what would happen.

The day before we are due to depart for the airport, my mother gets an unexpected visitor. It's my uncle Victor. He has come to the empty house in Reparto Mañana to say goodbye. My uncle, whom we never see because he now rarely visits Banes, is tall and even though he is older than my mother, he looks quite fit to me. He doesn't have a beard any more but his skin is bronzed, which I imagine is the result of spending too much time in the sun preparing his troops to defend the Revolution. My uncle has come on his own and to my surprise he is not wearing his army uniform, which is how I always picture him when I think about him. Instead, he is wearing civilian clothes and looks just like any other Habanero. He hasn't come in his government car either, taking the bus instead, which surprises me even more because everyone knows that the buses are always crowded and late.

Now that my uncle is here, my mother apologises for not being able to offer him anything to drink. Not even a *cafecito*, she says, as if this really was her house. The truth is, there isn't even a comfortable chair to sit on so they just stand there in the middle of this empty living room in this empty house in Reparto Mañana and say goodbye. It's the last time my mother will see her brother and as they hug each other before he departs, I can tell that she is trying desperately not to cry. Then my uncle is gone.

★

Today we leave Cuba. That's the plan, anyway, but of course in Cuba nothing ever goes according to plan, and there is nothing you can do about it. The Iberia flight between Havana and Madrid leaves mid-morning but we have been told to be at the Jose Martí International Airport, which is just outside Havana, at six so we have plenty of time for the *papeleo*, the paperwork. We arrive at the airport on schedule, but it becomes clear as soon as we walk in that the airport is pretty empty and that there is not much to do but wait.

Getting to the airport itself has been touch and go because it's not as if there is a long line of taxis parked out on the street to take *gusanos* to catch their plane to Madrid. Petrol is scarce, *compañero*, and tightly rationed, so taxis are nonexistent, which is why everyone queues for hours to get on a bus, hoping against all hope that the driver makes it to their destination without running out of petrol along the way, or the bus breaking down. Somehow, however, the ever-reliable Olmer has found someone to take us to the airport. It's a friend of a friend of a friend from Oriente province who owns an ancient American car and who has managed to save enough petrol coupons to be able to make a run to the airport and back—and who wants one hundred Cuban *pesos* for the trip, which is a lot of money but which my father is happy to pay since, in truth, he has little choice.

The money is exchanged indirectly, under the table, because in socialist Cuba, where we are busy building the New Man, you are not supposed to be paying people money like this for a taxi. There is no black market in Cuba, so we are told that if the police stop the car and ask what is going on, we must say that we are related to the driver, which would be a plausible story until the taxi that isn't a taxi arrives and the driver steps out, and we see with our very own eyes that he is a short black man. He is so old I think he must have been a taxi driver *antes del Triunfo*.

He politely nods his head in acknowledgement and then helps us pack the car with the old suitcases my parents have kept in storage for years and spruced up in the past few days just for this very occasion. Then my parents, my brother and I, my aunt Nidia and my aunt Mary and my cousins all pile as best we can into the old Chevrolet. It's like being inside a can of sardines, says my aunt Mary, but apart from that joke no one says much during the trip, not even my aunt Nidia, which is a surprise. Perhaps they are all saving their conversation for the airport.

My mother, my aunts, my cousins and my brother and I are sitting on hard plastic chairs in the terminal while my father goes over to the big desk with a sign that says Immigration to start the *papeleo*. But instead of spending an hour going through the papers as I expected, my father is now walking back to us and I can see as he gets closer that something is definitely wrong. He looks pale. All I can think of is that my aunt Nidia has done something silly or said something critical of Fidel and we are now being kept back in Cuba for another two years as punishment, which means my father will have to go back to cutting sugarcane for the Revolution and I will have to go back to school.

When he finally reaches us, my father says quietly, We are not leaving today. We aren't? No, he says, the plane is full and there are no seats left. My mother doesn't understand and neither do I. How can the plane be full? It's a capitalist plane, not a Havana bus! We are not leaving today, my father repeats, we have to go back to Reparto Mañana and wait until the Iberia flight next Tuesday. So close and yet so far.

I can tell it's going to be a long few days. Now the flight has been postponed, we are back at Reparto Mañana where Olmer has kindly agreed to allow us to stay—For as long as you need you can stay here, he says, and my parents don't know how to thank him enough. They are hoping it will only be for a few extra days but, really, who knows? The most obvious problem is food. My mother and my aunt Mary had brought food with them from Banes—pork sausages, pork chops, pork everything—but that is almost all gone since we expected to be in Madrid by now. We know we will have plenty to eat at the house of my cousin Eddi and her navy captain husband, but my father is reluctant to keep knocking on their door every day because he doesn't want to do anything that might compromise our relatives. I am not too worried because I know that whatever else happens, my mother will always find food for her boys. And anyway, we are in Havana! How difficult can it be?

For the next few days my father spends his time finalising the paperwork—the endless paperwork—that will eventually allow us to get on that elusive plane. We are so close . . . My father has to confirm flights again, ensure there are no other hiccups, that there are seats on the plane this time around. He visits the Spanish Embassy to make sure the visas are still all right and, most important of all, he goes methodically through every piece of paper necessary, every single Cuban document, to make sure it's all there because these are the very documents that will allow us to walk up the steps into the plane. He can't leave anything to chance. Chance has not been helpful so far.

You can tell it's a tough time for my father. He is more anxious than I have ever seen him before. Sometimes at the end of a long day, when we sit talking to my cousin Eddi and her family in her home, I can see his hands shaking, and I can understand why. When you are a *gusano*, nothing is for sure. At any moment, without any warning, the police can turn up and tell us we are not going anywhere. They don't need much of an excuse to keep us here. All that really needs to happen is for someone in authority in Banes to decide that something is missing from my father's file, or even from my own file, and it's goodbye Spain. Nothing is a given, not until the Iberia plane is in the sky, and even then, my friends have warned me, the Cuban government can demand that the plane be turned around and that the *gusanos* on board be kept in Cuba for a little while longer. Apparently it's happened before, although I don't know how my friends know this since I have never ever read in *Granma* or heard on the radio about people leaving Cuba. But I know that at any moment we can be stopped. No wonder my father is a nervous wreck.

Meanwhile, my mother, my brother and my aunts play tourists in Havana, even though we soon discover there are no tourists at all in Havana. Not real tourists. Not since Fidel announced some years ago that tourism was a capitalist plot invented by the rich imperialists to enslave and exploit the poor. No more tourists, *El Maxímo Líder* has said, because when we last had hundreds of thousands of tourists *antes del Triunfo*, they were Americans and Europeans who came to Havana not because it was a beautiful city but because they wanted to exploit Cubans, mix with the *lumpen*, take drugs, sleep with our women and spend their time in casinos owned by the Mafia. The Revolution put a stop to all that, closed the casinos, stopped building flashy capitalist hotels, closed the country clubs and the golf courses and turned all those tourist planes back.

The only tourists we see in Havana are visitors—they are not called tourists at all but *compañeros* or *camaradas*—who come to see first hand the great achievements of the Revolution and who spend time not in the brothels or bars or gambling houses that no longer exist but visiting cement factories outside Havana or new schools in the countryside or even cutting some sugarcane somewhere in Las Villas province, a very tangible demonstration of their support for the Revolution.

Some of these visitors come from capitalist countries, even from the United States. I know because whenever they arrive and whatever they do, Cuban television cameras will follow them up and down the island, and then, at night on the news, they show these capitalist friends of Cuba happily posing with *campesinos* or factory workers and saying what a great leader Fidel is and, yes, how lucky we are to live in socialist Cuba. They always smile for the cameras when they say this, which is nice of them. Then they jump back on their capitalist planes and go back to their capitalist homes.

Most of the visitors we see in Havana—at the Havana zoo, the Vedado neighbourhood or at the aquarium—come from fraternal countries like the Soviet Union, the German Democratic Republic or from Hungary. You can tell them from far away, my mother says, because they all look so *tosco*, by which she means they look nothing like Cubans: they are blonde, have pink skin and short, spiky haircuts like the haircuts you get in the army, wear loud shirts and carry bulky Praktica cameras around their necks. The women always wear sandals too, and sometimes hats to protect themselves from the strong Cuban sun, and if you look closely, you can tell that many of them don't shave under their armpits, which is definitely not the way Cuban women would walk around in public, Revolution or no Revolution.

A friend of mine in Banes told me that the Russians who come to Cuba live in special apartment blocks, away from the Cubans, and they have their own doctors and even their own shops where they can buy anything they want—even meat!—without having to stand in line. I think there is another reason you can tell them apart: they walk around in groups and sometimes it seems as if they own the place, which in a way they do, although I don't know this yet. When I get to Spain I will read for the first time that following the collapse of the Cuban economy in

1969–70, when the entire island was diverted to cut sugarcane for the *zafra de los diez millones*, the Russians told Fidel that enough was enough. They insisted that if they were going to continue providing Cuba with billions of dollars in aid, then the Cuban economy had to be centralised along Soviet lines. To make sure this happened, Moscow sent 10 000 technicians and advisers to Cuba to run the country. That's a lot of technicians and advisers. That's why we see so many of them walking around Havana, the men taking pictures of old buildings and the women exposing their unshaved armpits.

In truth, there is not much for us *guajiros* from Banes to do in Havana during the week once we have been to the zoo and the aquarium and then spent time pointing at the groups of East Germans. We have been to the cinema but they are showing the same movies we have already seen in Banes. We have been window-shopping around the Vedado area, but there is nothing much in the windows to look at. Not that the windows are left empty. Instead of clothes or cooking pots or books being displayed, they have revolutionary slogans or colourful paintings depicting heroic Vietnamese guerrillas using chopsticks to gouge out the eyes of the imperialist enemy.

Out of curiosity, we walk into one of the stores which my aunt Nidia says, with certainty, used to be El Encanto, the most famous and glamorous department store in all of Cuba *antes del Triunfo*. I don't think my aunt is right because I remember reading in my history books back at school that El Encanto had been burned down some years ago by counter-revolutionaries working for the CIA, but I don't say anything. It doesn't pay to argue with my aunt Nidia. If there is anything she doesn't like it is a smarty-pants boy telling her she got her department stores mixed up . . . Whatever this shop is called, it is huge, with long aisles and lots of glass cabinets and glass display cases. They are all empty or they have only a few goods on display, things no one seems to need or want, which is much as we expected. It's quiet in here, too, except for two women of indeterminate age—they seem old to me—standing behind the counter gossiping. They look at us as we walk past them and they can tell almost immediately that we are *guajiros* from Oriente because they give us a tight, insincere smile and then go back to their gossiping.

It seems my mother and my aunt Mary are slowly solving the food problem. Because there is nothing to cook with, my aunt has been down the road to a hardware shop and somehow managed to convince the shop assistant to sell her—on the quiet, of course—the only container they have in the shop: a large enamel chamber pot. This is what my mother and my aunt now use to fry green plantains in. I think it looks funny, even when my aunt assures everyone the chamber pot is brand new. It hasn't been used, she insists. Still, she can't convince my aunt Nidia, who simply refuses to eat anything from it, saying something about, How low have we sunk, *¡Dios Mio!*

We also eat spaghetti. Almost every day. There is nothing wrong with spaghetti, don't get me wrong, but it's not what you'd call a typically Cuban dish—not even when you add some extra garlic—and even if it was, it's probably not the type of food you'd want to eat day after day. But as my mother says, it's either spaghetti or we go hungry. To get the spaghetti, my mother and my aunt Mary go out every afternoon and queue outside one of a handful of take-away places the Revolution has opened across Havana in the past few months. Each serves just one dish: spaghetti, already cooked in a rich red sauce that is supposed to have tomatoes and meat in it but when you look closely seems to be just tomato.

My aunt Nidia says it's the new food of the Revolution, spaghetti for breakfast, lunch and dinner. They want to turn us into Italians! she says, laughing, and my mother tells her to be quiet, stop talking nonsense and eat because there is nothing else in the cupboards that line the small kitchen in the empty house in Reparto Mañana. To my brother and me, normally very fussy eaters, the spaghetti seems exciting at first because no one cooks or sells spaghetti in Banes but by the second night, the novelty has well and truly worn off.

The only other food that seems to be freely available all over Havana—and in plentiful supply—is *merluza*, or hake. Every fish shop in the city sells hake, according to my father, who likes his fish. Nothing else is available in the fish shops apart from hake. It's the way things work in Cuba: no one can explain why there is so much hake around but equally no one is complaining because you can buy as much as you want without needing to use your ration book. This is exactly what my father has done, so there are several kilograms of hake squashed into my cousin Eddi's refrigerator as he dreams up ever more inventive ways to cook hake. It makes a change from spaghetti.

My aunt Adelina has come to Havana too, along with my uncle Rogelio, her husband, in theory so my uncle can see a specialist—he is not well—but in truth so that they can say goodbye to us. They are staying at the house of my cousin Roger, who is my uncle's son from his first marriage, back in the days when Rogelio worked for an American company and lived in the United States. Then he came back to Cuba and gave all his children English names. Like Roger. I am not close to my cousin Roger because he is older than I am and for many years he has lived in Havana where he is an up and coming academic at the University of Havana. When we visit his house later in the week I discover he is also writing a book, which makes me think this is by far the most sophisticated thing anyone can do here in Cuba in 1971. His home in Havana is not huge but it's in a quiet neighbourhood with trees at the front and room for residents to park their Russian cars. My father says immediately that it is a neighbourhood for people who are well connected, which is what he says about anyone in Cuba who has a Russian car.

Inside, the house is full of books and papers and has framed prints on the walls, and Roger and his wife, whom I had not met before, have lots of friends who are just like them, young and sophisticated, at least to my eyes. They sit around in the living room discussing important issues and talking about their next visit to Moscow or Berlin to attend academic conferences because, unlike most Cubans, my cousin and his friends are allowed to travel overseas every now and then. They are allowed to peek outside and even to visit capitalist countries but never, it seems to me, with their families. They always travel in groups but never, ever, with their wives or husbands, let alone their children. That may be why they always come back.

Before we leave my uncle Rogelio, who is the most meticulous member of our extended family, brings out a camera that I assume must belong to Roger. It looks like one of those bulky East German cameras that Fidel gives you if you are a good revolutionary or a Hero of Labour, but I am not sure. We all pose outside the house on the small lawn area, my brother and I sporting our fresh *malanguitas* haircuts and my mother wearing her big sunglasses that make her look almost European. These will be our last photographs in Cuba.

23 · *ADIOS*, CUBA

We leave the house at Reparto Mañana at five o'clock on the day we are about to leave Cuba—unless we get sent back from the airport again. You never know, says my aunt Nidia, which makes my father even more anxious than he already is. It's the not knowing that is killing him, I can tell. I know what he is going through because in the pit of my stomach I feel sick too, but I keep it to myself. I figure my parents have plenty to worry about already. Anyway, I don't know what we will do if we get sent back from the airport. I think we have had enough of spaghetti and hake and wouldn't it be great to sleep on a real bed again and not on an old American car seat? I am tired of the old car seat. My neck hurts and my arms and my stomach and my chest area are blotchy and itchy. When can I sleep in a real bed again? These are guilt-soaked, counter-revolutionary, bourgeois questions, I know, but my arms and my stomach are really, really itchy . . .

We are picked up by the same driver who took us to the airport last week. He's driving the same old American car and my father pays another hundred *pesos*, no complaints, and then we all do the sardine trick again and squash back into the taxi that isn't, and then we are on our way. No one says much during the trip this time either, but I can tell what everyone is thinking: is this it? Are we really leaving today?

Outside, it is still dark. The street lights are on even though you can tell that it won't be long before the sun starts to rise and turn night into another hot, bright Cuban day. The old Chevrolet with the rickety seats and the cloudy rear-view mirror splatters along streets that are almost completely deserted, except for the occasional army jeep speeding by, always in a hurry, ready to defend the Revolution. We drive past darkened government buildings that are ten storeys high, some with huge posters of Fidel, Camilo and Che looking defiant and heroic, which is exactly how revolutionaries are supposed to look. There is a giant billboard on the route encouraging Cubans—other Cubans, I am sure, not *gusanos* like us—to become better revolutionaries, ready to fight against imperialism. We are not afraid of you Americans, the billboard says, as if daring that evil Richard Nixon to invade Cuba. *Patria o Muerte¡ Venceremos!* says another one. Fatherland or Death. We shall win!

As we drive past apartment blocks that are only now beginning to wake up, I notice small groups of people barely visible in the dark, standing in queues—even at this hour!— waiting for the bus that will take them to work. I roll down the window and stick my head out of the old car and I swear I can smell the sea in the air and hear the waves in the distance. I am sure I can taste the salt in the light dawn breeze, but maybe I'm imagining things. Get your head back inside the car, my mother yells, what do you want to do? Get yourself killed and give me a *patatu*?

You can tell it's going to be another warm, sunny day, this first day of March. It's spring in Havana, for sure, but all Cuban days seem to be warm and sunny. Or at least that is the way I will always remember them. It's probably just like any other start to the day in Havana with people up there in the apartment blocks only now waking up, making themselves a *cafecito* for breakfast. Perhaps a chunk of bread dipped in a mixture of oil, salt and a crushed garlic clove before setting off to work. Another day in revolutionary Cuba. But not for us.

When we get to the airport, it is almost empty again, and I don't think it's got anything to do with the fact that it's really early in the morning. We are wearing our best (and only) travelling outfits—*el traje de salir de Cuba*. Both my brother and I are wearing suits made for us over a year ago by a tailor in Banes, a friend of my father's, from the only heavy material my mother could find, a thick, grey, woollen material, probably from East Germany, that makes my brother and me very uncomfortable because it's getting hotter all the time. It's itchy in this suit and we think we look stupid, but my mother insisted because she says you only leave Cuba once and we want to arrive in Madrid—will we ever arrive?—looking our best. You know, there is no point arguing with your mother when she is determined like that.

My father tells us to go and find seats, just like he did last week, and then he walks over to the Immigration desk, the same desk where a *miliciano* told him just five or six days ago that there were no spare seats on the Iberia plane and sent him back home to Reparto Mañana. Surely they are not going to do this to him a second time? From where we are sitting I can tell my father is nervous because he is tapping his right foot and fidgeting. Oh God, that little voice is saying inside my head, let's get this over with. I don't know how long it takes because I don't have a watch, but it feels like long, agonising hours before my father turns around and walks over to us and says, with just a hint of a smile, we have seats. At this stage these are the sweetest words in the entire language.

We say goodbye to my aunt Mary and my cousins for what we all think will be the last time ever. It involves much hugging, crying and promises to write and to phone, if we can, as soon as we get to Madrid. Then my aunt Nidia, my parents, and my brother and I walk to the end of a corridor where a *miliciano* politely opens the door and ushers us into another section of the airport. It is a kind of reverse customs post where instead of inspecting the luggage of incoming visitors, uniformed immigration officers ask *gusanos* leaving the country to open up all their luggage so it can be inspected, piece by piece.

The immigration official inspecting our suitcases is probably in his twenties. He wears an olive green uniform like almost everyone of any authority in Cuba and I can tell he is polite but thorough, unpacking every single piece of clothing and then, with great care, feeling around the inside of the suitcases searching for I don't know what. Hidden treasure? We are not even allowed to take money with us. I know my mother has spent a lot of time packing up and trying to squeeze as much as she can into these suitcases that carry everything we own, but neither she nor my father nor my aunt Nidia say anything as the inspection continues, item by item. They pretend it's the most natural thing in the world. I guess they are just glad to get the ordeal over and done with, so we stand there and wait until the cases are fully inspected and the clothes bundled back inside and the cases locked again and set aside to be taken into the hold of the plane. We hope.

Then we go back to our seats and wait. It's like everything else in Cuba: you have to sit and wait or, more often, stand up and wait. There are other families like ours waiting too, and all the mothers must be like my mother because everyone is wearing their best we-are-leaving-Cuba outfits: men in suits that are too tight, women wearing dresses that are way out of date, young girls with pretty ribbons in their hair and boys like my brother and me, forced to wear hot, itchy suits made from what I am sure is material for Arctic blankets.

The long corridors I can see from where I am are polished and sparkling clean—and empty. Apart from our group of a hundred or more very nervous *gusanos* the only people I can see are a small group of obviously very important visitors who walk past and point at us and then ask questions of the man who is guiding them. I can't hear what they are saying but they are probably Chilean *compañeros* visiting Cuba for the first time now that Chile has a socialist president who has become Fidel's new best friend.

There are plenty of *milicianos* around, standing guard, guns at the ready but looking bored. You can tell they are keeping an eye on our group in case we do something stupid, like try to smuggle out precious gold or diamonds that were kept hidden from *antes del Triunfo* and which now belong to the People. Every now and then a young airport office worker walks past, with chocolate-coloured skin and long, dark curly hair, swinging her hips like Cuban women do, and she stops to flirt with one of the *milicianos* and then she keeps walking, not even looking at us, just walking somewhere. Once the flirting is over, the *miliciano* goes back to looking bored.

I am not sure how long we have been waiting because I have stopped asking my mother what time is it. Both she and my father are jumpy, especially my father, who is sweating a little, and looking uncomfortable in his suit. He wipes his forehead with a white cotton handkerchief—his best handkerchief—that has been kept untouched, brand new, for this very occasion. His we-are-leaving-Cuba handkerchief. He is wearing his we-are-leaving-Cuba shoes, too. He bought them just before he was sent to the labour camp to cut sugarcane for the Revolution three years ago but they are now too tight. He says they are so tight he thinks he won't be able to walk very far with them when we get to Madrid.

Hear that? He said, when . . . My mother says we will worry about that when we get there. When we get there! For the first time I am beginning to believe they might just be right. Before we left for the airport, my father told my brother and me to behave. No running around, no talking out loud, no silly stunts, he said, although I could tell that he was really referring to my aunt Nidia. She's really what worries my father. But his instructions were clear: on your best behaviour. This is difficult at the best of times let alone when you have been waiting for so long, and you are wearing an itchy suit and your parents are so nervous they snap at you at the slightest provocation, telling you to sit back down and keep quiet and stop fidgeting, and *coño*, stop kicking your brother.

We sit there and look out the glass windows but there is not much action outside, either. On the tarmac I can count only a handful of planes, including a couple of propeller airplanes that belong to Cubana, the Cuban airline. My father says, quietly, that they are old Soviet planes given to Cuba as a gift by our fraternal cousins in Moscow. He then whispers, I bet those planes are so old and in such poor condition, they can't fly. Then, a little further out on the tarmac, beyond the Cubana planes, I spot the plane we have been waiting for. It's a large jet with red stripes and that magic word: Iberia. It's our plane—the weekly Iberia flight that takes *gusanos* like us to Spain, and let me tell you, it is a beautiful sight. We are so close. I keep thinking, they are not going to turn us back again, are they?

While I am looking at the planes, a *miliciana* comes over to where my parents and my aunt Nidia are sitting and talks to them quietly. Next thing I know, my mother and my aunt are being led away by the uniformed policewoman and they disappear into a room off to one side. We don't know what's going on. It won't take long, the *miliciana* said, just come with us, please. It won't take long . . . But my mind is racing because all I can think is that something bad must have happened. That voice inside my head is saying, Something is wrong; you and your father and your brother will be allowed to leave Cuba but your mother will be kept behind. I can hear my father trying to reassure my brother and me, but I am still scared. The little voice inside my head says, Please, God, don't let them take my mother away. I can tell my father is cursing under his breath; he is adamant my aunt Nidia must have said something counter-revolutionary while in the toilet, probably when talking to another *gusano* in there, and doesn't she know that every room in this airport is bugged? Every room in Cuba is bugged, *coño*! Even the toilets!

We sit and wait for what seems like at least half an hour. It's the worst half-hour I think I am ever going to experience. Then, finally, I see my mother and my aunt reappear from the room, on the other side of the glass, waving at us, and it's the most comforting sight I can imagine. It's all right, my mother says when she returns to our seats, but I can tell it isn't. For reasons that will remain a mystery my mother and my aunt were picked out of the group of *gusanos* for a full body search, taken to a small room off one of the corridors and told to undress completely. Stark naked. Then, my mother whispers to my father, they were searched by two *milicianas*. They searched everywhere, my aunt Nidia says cryptically. *¡Nos revisaron todo!* my mother confirms, and I can tell she feels angry and violated and totally humiliated. It's not the way she wanted to leave her homeland. So, we all just sit back down, not saying anything.

★

As we walk out onto the deserted tarmac I am mesmerised by the shiny jet from Iberia which sits there in the distance, majestic, like a huge, exotic European bird that got lost and ended up landing here, almost melting in the tropical Cuban sun.

We walk in single file because that is what we have been told to do, except my brother and I are holding on to my mother's hands and every step we take towards the plane's step-ladder is a step that seems to take forever. All I can think of is the advice my friend Pepito gave me back in Banes before we left: Don't look back. Whatever you do, don't look back, or they will think you don't want to leave Cuba and they will keep you here, and your parents will go on to Spain but you ... *tú te quedas*. You will stay here.

I keep repeating the message in my mind: Don't look back. Don't look back. Don't look back. But I do. I can't help myself. For just a micro-second I turn my head around and look back, because I am leaving Cuba for good, I am leaving behind the rest of my family and my home and my friends and everybody else, and how can I not look back just once? Not that there is much to see. A small group of people on the distant terrace, bunched together, waving goodbye but not saying anything, or not saying anything I can hear above the sound of the jet engines of the Iberia plane. I can't even tell if one of the people waving goodbye is my aunt Mary but as I turn around, just for that brief moment, I realise that there is a part of me that doesn't want to go. Despite what my parents say, despite what they have told everyone, despite what I have been saying. I am scared. I know that I can stay if I want to. All I have to do is say so to the *milicianos* I can see at the bottom of the plane steps.

I keep walking, holding tight to my mother, sweating now

227

because I am sure that having disobeyed everyone and looked back—despite what my parents and my friends all said—I am convinced that just as I reach those steps, one of the *milicianos* will put his hand on my shoulders and say, That's all right, *compañerito*, I saw you looking back, which means you don't want to leave Cuba, and that is all right, you can stay . . .

24 · IN A PLANE OF PLENTY

This, I hear my father say as he points to the fine china plate sitting on the tray in front of him, is lobster. And as he says the Spanish word for lobster—*langosta*—he smacks his lips . . . I can tell he is going to enjoy his meal. I have half a lobster sitting on a plate on my tray, too, staring at me like some strange creature from the bottom of the sea. It has been cut in two and then covered in a thick cream that my father swears is melted cheese. Try it, he says across the aisle. You will like it, he promises, but I barely touch it. I am not hungry.

We are flying high up above the clouds somewhere over the Atlantic Ocean. It's been at least three hours since the plane took off from Havana and I am sitting by the window, next to my mother and my aunt Nidia, while my father and my brother are just across the aisle. I can tell from here that my brother, who is even more of a fussy eater than I am, is not impressed with his lobster either. Perhaps he is not hungry. Perhaps he is also thinking, like I am, that he has just left his friends behind in Banes and he is going to miss them a lot, no matter what our mother says. No amount of capitalist food is going to make us feel better.

My father, on the other hand, seems to be impressed. He sits there enjoying his lobster and the potato salad that came in a small side dish and when the air hostess asks him, What would you like to drink with your meal, sir?, he looks at her, smiles and replies, *Señorita, lo que tenga.* Whatever you've got, Miss, which is why she has brought over a whole bottle of wine, Spanish wine so red it is the colour of blood, I swear. My father tastes it with great care and declares it to be *muy bueno*—very good. Later, before they take away the trays and bring dessert, he will eat my portion of lobster and half of my brother's. It's been a while since he has eaten with so much satisfaction and when everything is cleared away he stretches back in the seat, which is too small for someone of his size, and for a moment there he looks like a very satisfied *gusano*.

All this is a world away from Havana, and very different even from Jose Martí International Airport. When we walked up the metal stairs into the belly of what seemed to me like the biggest plane in the world, I could tell most of the other *gusanos* had not been on a plane before either, because they kept saying things like, My God! This is a really big plane! Some women were sobbing and using their best we-are-leaving-Cuba handkerchiefs to wipe away the tears, but everyone else was respectfully quiet, which is highly unusual for Cubans at any time. It's as if no one wanted to say or do anything, nothing at all, that might have encouraged the *milicianos*, who were still guarding the bottom of the stairs, to come up and escort you back down. I don't know if this ever happens but back in Banes my friend Pepito swore to me that his mother has heard of *gusanos* being marched down the plane—even after they put their seatbelts on!—because their papers were not in order or something equally serious. It's true, he said. Sometimes they even turn the plane back!

So, we enter the plane and find our seats, strap our seatbelts on as we are told to and then sit there sweating, because it's very hot, waiting patiently for the rest of the passengers to come on board. Finally, once the doors are locked, the air hostesses walk to the middle of the aisles and as the plane starts to move forward, slowly at first, they give a quick demonstration of what we must do if there is an emergency. I can see that my mother doesn't like this one bit. Inside her head, I am sure, she is already picturing the Iberia jet faltering mid-sky and then plunging into the Atlantic. I take one final look through the small window but the airport terminal is too far away now for me to confirm whether my aunt Mary and my cousins are still there, standing in the hot, tropical sun waving us goodbye. In case they are, I wave.

Now the plane is rushing down the runway so fast it is shaking inside, which is quite scary, especially when this is your first plane trip ever. It's only when the plane finally takes off that I notice my mother has shut her eyes and is holding on to the armrest as if her life depended on it. It makes me feel a bit better because it proves she is as scared as I am, no matter what she says. As the plane gains altitude and all I can see of Cuba is a diminishing speck of land surrounded entirely by a brilliant blue sea, the little light above the seats goes 'ping', meaning you can undo your seatbelt, stretch your legs or go to the bathroom.

Right on cue, as soon as the little light goes off, there is this great communal sigh of relief inside the plane and everyone on board, I swear, starts talking at once and waving their arms around and acting just like normal Cubans. *Por fin*, I can hear my father say to no one in particular. At last. And his face is the face of a man who can finally relax—no matter what happens next, he is not being sent back to Cuba.

Later, the air hostesses come around with a tray of cigarettes. American cigarettes. I watch my father light up, take a deep puff, look at the cigarette in his hand—This is a Chesterfield, he says to my mother across the aisle—and then give a little smile because it has been a long time since he had a capitalist cigarette and capitalist cigarettes taste a lot better, he says, than Cuban socialist cigarettes, which are called *Populares* and have no filter and precious little tobacco inside their thin paper wrappers. I know what this means. It means that from now until the end of time my parents will compare everything to how it used to be in Cuba, for better or worse. After dinner, when they dim the lights and the plane goes quiet again, or as quiet as you can expect of a planeload of Cubans, I look out the window and all I can see is darkness. The void is surprising because I am sure we haven't been flying all that long and I am pretty sure it must still be sunny in Cuba. It's always sunny in Cuba.

If you come closer to where I am, right here by the window, and look down, you can see Madrid. At least I think it is Madrid. Thousands and thousands of little points of light blink on and off hypnotically. As we get closer, the lights get brighter and within minutes the plane starts to descend. My ears pop (what's going on here?), and then we land on the tarmac with a huge thud that shakes everything and everyone inside the Iberia jet. Some of the *gusanos* on board clap when the plane touches down, or they make the sign of the cross, which is not very revolutionary, I know, but which makes me think they must be just as relieved as my mother is that we are now, finally, on firm ground. Or maybe they are just happy to be in Spain.

Like my parents, I am pretty excited to have landed in Madrid but I am as nervous as I think they must be about what awaits us in Spain. My parents know a handful of families who used to live in Banes and have since settled in Spain but we have no relatives here and no idea what Madrid is like, how to get around the city, let alone where to go to find work, which my father says will be his number one priority. In the longer-term, our plan is to apply to migrate to the United States and join my aunt and uncle in New York as soon as possible. It's what most Cubans do when they leave Cuba, no matter where they go: they make their way to the United States, preferably to Miami, which is hot and steamy and bright just like Cuba. Except they have air conditioning. In truth, we have no idea how long we will have to wait in Spain or how we will manage. We don't have any money with us although we know my aunt Mirta in New York has cabled money to a family friend, Nora, who is from Banes and is now living in Madrid with her two daughters. They are supposed to be at the airport waiting for us. If they're not, it's going to be a bit awkward.

As we get ushered into the terminal, we all notice just how cold it is. It's March. In fact, the coldest March for years, as we discover later, and the suits my mother had made for my brother and me and which we hated so much because they were hot and itchy in Havana are now useless against the cold. *Madre mía*, my mother says, worried that her tropical children will catch a cold and then develop pneumonia or some other just as dangerous capitalist disease. It must be quite a sight, this planeload of Cuban *gusanos*, happy and sad at the same time for having left their homeland and now exposed to the brutally cold reality of what is supposed to be a European spring. *¡Madre mía, que frío!* Talk about cold! But I am too busy just looking around me to notice the cold. It's truly like another world in the terminal. A huge room with people everywhere, even though I am sure it must be well past midnight. The lights are bright and there is this funny, humming kind of noise which I soon realise is the sound of people rushing past on the way to somewhere else.

As my father collects our old suitcases so we can go through Customs and Immigration, we spot our friend Nora on the other side, waving at us. I swear I can almost hear my father relax. There is much hugging and welcoming and questions about Banes and, How are things in Cuba? *Malísimamente mal.* Really bad, is the obvious reply. And then she hands my father a big fat envelope full of big, colourful notes, thousands and thousands of Spanish *pesetas,* which makes me think—wrongly, as it turns out—that we must now be capitalist millionaires or at least members of what Fidel calls the bourgeoisie. Then, suitcases at the ready, we and the rest of the *gusanos* are directed to buses that wait outside, where it is really, really cold, for the trip into Madrid and in particular to the Migration Offices where all Cubans must go to register on arrival and be provided with whatever assistance the Spanish government can offer. In our case, a hotel room would be a good start.

It's warm inside the bus, which smells new and is shiny and nothing like those old American buses back in Cuba, and everyone talks at once, asking each other, Do you have anyone waiting for you here in Madrid? One woman keeps crying quietly because she already misses her family in Cuba, and I hope she stops soon because otherwise I am sure my mother will start crying too and that, I can tell you, is not a happy thing when you have just landed in Madrid. Someone else passes around a bottle of wine that was given to them by one of the air hostesses, *¡Que Dios la bendiga!* God bless her. It's strange how you can make friends so quickly and so easily with people you have just met.

My eyes are glued to the big windows of the bus because I can't believe how many cars and buses there are on the road, even at this time of night. Haven't these people heard of petrol rationing? As we drive into the centre of the city there are even more cars and we go past fountains made of white marble that spout water jets high up into the sky, and there are enormous billboards with flashing lights. To my surprise, they are advertising soft drinks and refrigerators and banks and there is not a single revolutionary slogan to be seen. There is no *Patria o Muerte ¡Venceremos!* anywhere. Then there are the shop windows all lit up and full of stuff. Toys, food, clothes. It looks decadent and rich and imperialist and nothing, I tell you, nothing at all like Cuba. My aunt Nidia keeps pointing, *Mira, mira eso* . . . Look, look there, directing my eyes to another shop window full of stuff. I think there is just too much to take in one go. I wonder if this is how the capitalists capture your mind and corrupt your heart, with all these glittering prizes that no self respecting socialist would want.

When we get to the Migration Centre in General Sanjurjo Street in Madrid there are Spanish officials waiting to place big stamps on our passports, and others, Spaniards and Cubans like us, who help you find accommodation for the night. The place is packed, as you would expect, and yes, we need to queue although this time none of the *gusanos* seems to mind too much. My brother and I are dead tired and all I want is a bed. Please . . . get me a bed. It's then that I see my parents rush to a tall, skinny man with glasses and what looks like a very expensive, very counter-revolutionary overcoat, who appears to have been waiting for us. I don't know who this man is but my parents obviously do and his presence there, of all places, appears to them as nothing short of a miracle. His name, I am about to discover, is Enriquito Martínez, and he owned the pharmacy just up the street from my parents' shop. He was one of my father's closest friends in Banes until he and his wife Armentina and his whole family left for the United States in 1960. They haven't seen each other for eleven years.

It's a miracle, my mother keeps saying, sounding incredulous—and she is right. Enriquito and his family now live in Madrid, where he has a prosperous export business, and he heard from mutual friends in the United States that we were on our way.

Now he is here, waiting for us like a guardian angel, which makes me think that perhaps this is my reward for going to Sunday mass in Banes all that time rather than to the cinema. Enriquito is telling my parents that he has rented a room for us in a hotel for the next few days and tomorrow, he says to my father, we will look for an apartment. Everything is all right now, *chico*, you are in Madrid. The communists can't get you any more. Everything will be fine . . .

While Enriquito the miracle-maker waits to take us to the hotel, my father queues to get his papers signed and finalised. And because he is Cuban and this is what happens when you are Cuban, he reaches the head of the queue and finds that the man who is at the desk sorting out the paperwork is someone he knows. His name is Francisco and he is from Holguin, the city where my father lived as a young man. Now my father is talking to Francisco as if they have known each other forever, which they probably have, and then my father calls us all over, including my aunt Nidia, so we can say hello too.

All I want is to go to bed because now I am really tired but Francisco just keeps talking. Migrating to the United States won't be easy, he is telling my parents as he sorts out the paperwork. You know, there is a long wait, probably two years, because there is only a limited number of visas every year for Cubans. And it's not easy to find good jobs here in Spain when you are an exile, you know. If you want my advice, he says—not waiting to see whether we do, because he is Cuban and Cubans give you advice even when you don't ask for it—my advice is to go somewhere else instead of *El Norte*. Go to a place that needs migrants; a place with a great future, where they welcome you with open arms. If it wasn't for the fact that my wife is in Cuba and I am waiting to get permission for her to leave, I'd pack up my bags tomorrow, he adds.

What are you talking about? my father asks Francisco. What's this place?

Australia, *mi socio*, Francisco says. Go to Australia.

That's another story. Now, I just want to go to bed.